D1253602

TWO CONCEPTS OF THE RULE OF LAW

By the same author

Über Formulierung der Menschenrechte (1956)
The Federalist: A Classic on Federalism and Free Government (1960)
In Defense of Property (1963)
Magna Carta and Property (1965)
America's Political Dilemma: From Limited to Unlimited Democracy (1968)
Youth, University and Democracy (1970)
Bedeutungswandel der Menschenrechte (1971)
Academic Truths and Frauds (1972)

TWO CONCEPTS
OF THE RULE OF LAW

by

GOTTFRIED DIETZE

LIBERTY FUND, INC. · INDIANAPOLIS · 1973

Chapters One and Two were originally published in German in Karl
Dietrich Bracher, Christopher Dawson, Willi Geiger, Rudolf Smend,
eds., in collaboration with Hans-Justus Rinck, *Die moderne Demo-
kratie und ihr Recht: Modern Constitutionalism and Democracy*
Festschrift für Gerhard Leibholz (J. C. B. Mohr [Paul Siebeck]
Tübingen, 1966) and Klaus von Beyme, ed., *Theory and Politics:
Theorie und Politik*, Festschrift für Carl Joachim Friedrich (Martinus
Nijhoff, Haag, 1971).

FOR
CARL J. FRIEDRICH
AND
GERHARD LEIBHOLZ
FRIENDS OF THE RULE OF LAW

TABLE OF CONTENTS

PREFACE

This study concerns the freedom of the individual, the authority of the government, and their anarchic and despotic perversions.

While freedom and government have been considered opposites, the former generally is not safe without the latter. Free government implies that men be free and protected by their rulers. Liberty exists in, not without, an order. Individuals are willing to give up part of their freedom so that the government may secure the rest. Whereas men always should be wary of power and its threat to liberty, they also must recognize that legal authority is necessary for their protection from unlawful elements. As man is the measure of things, human freedom must be measured humanely by the law. In a free society, the following rule applies: the greater the regulation by the government, the greater the danger to freedom; the less regulation, the more imperative the strict enforcement of the laws.

However, even the rule of law is not without risks and problems, as the following pages will attempt to show.

Thanks are due to the Liberty Fund which encouraged the present study and stimulated it by seminars.

11 November, 1972   G. D.

TWO CONCEPTS OF THE RULE OF LAW

INTRODUCTION

FIFTY YEARS AGO, Albert Venn Dicey, the great exponent of the rule of law,[1] died. Today, we ask ourselves whether in the half-century following his death the rule of law he cherished has not also passed away.

There were threats to it from fascism, national socialism, and communism. Even Western democracies were not spared. In England, Lord Chief Justice Hewart in 1929 discussed the new despotism of administrative decrees.[2] In 1967, H. R. Hahlo bewailed the demise of the common law, considered by many the hard core of the rule of law.[3] In the United States, Raoul Desvernine denounced the democratic despotism of the New Deal in 1936.[4] Since World War II, people have asked whether the Constitution, generally considered to be basic to the rule of law, is still alive.[5]

To authoritarian challenges of the rule of law there

---

[1] A. V. Dicey, *Introduction to the Study of the Law of the Constitution* (1885; 2d ed. 1886; 3rd ed. 1889; 4th ed. 1893; 5th ed. 1897; 6th ed. 1902; 7th ed. 1908, 2 reprints 1920; 8th ed. 1915, reprints 1923, 1924, 1926, 1927, 1931; 9th ed. 1939, reprints 1941, 1945, 1948, 1950, 1952, 1956; 10th ed. 1959, reprinted 1960. Unless noted differently, references will be to the 10th edition.

[2] Lord Hewart, *The New Despotism* (1929).

[3] H. R. Hahlo, "Here Lies the Common Law: Rest in Peace," *Modern Law Review* XXX (1967) 241.

[4] Raoul E. Desvernine, *Democratic Despotism* (1936).

[5] See the author's *America's Political Dilemma* (1968).

3

have been added anarchical threats. Friends of the rule of law, so far seeing that rule threatened mainly by big government, now must fear that it is endangered as much by government impotence. The threat of permissiveness seems to be as comprehensive as that of big government. The past years have been characterized not only by headline-making riots, abductions, and blackmail, climaxed by the killing of hostages at the Olympic Games, but also by a widespread general disrespect for the law—all of which governments seem to be unable or unwilling to cope with.

Dicey would have deeply resented this development. An individualist of the liberal [6] era, law to him meant mainly the common law with its far-reaching protection of the individual. While he admitted the usefulness of statutes and administrative decrees,[7] he trusted they would reflect the spirit of the common law. The rule of law implied "the security given under the English constitution to the rights of individuals."[8] This emphasis upon freedom by no means signalled an inclination toward anarchism. Dicey favored the freedom of men from arbitrary government, not their freedom arbitrarily to defy the law. The rule of law not only provided for limitations upon the power of the state for the sake of the individual, but also for restrictions of individual license for the sake of society and those composing it. A liberal civilization presupposes a legal or-

[6] In this study, the terms "liberal" and "liberalism" will be used in their original sense, implying the freedom of the rights of the individual, including his property rights, from the government and state authority. The liberal state is thus a *laissez-faire* state in a wide sense.

[7] Dicey, *Law of the Constitution*, 52 f. Cf. F. H. Lawson, "Dicey Revisited," *Political Studies* VII (1959) 109, 220.

[8] Dicey, *Law of the Constitution* 184.

4

der. Characterized by the rule of law, the civilized state is an "orderly state"[9] protecting freedom by enforcing the law.

In the beginning of his introduction to the tenth edition of *The Law of the Constitution*, E. C. S. Wade wrote that Dicey's "warning of the danger of not paying 'sufficient attention to the law of the constitution as it now actually exists' is of even greater importance today." If this remark was justified in 1959, after big government had challenged constitutionalism, it must be even more relevant today when, in addition, we are experiencing an increasing negation of the law by those who seem to forget that civilized freedom is impossible without an enforcement of the laws.

Given the present interest in problems concerning freedom, law, and order, the author presents in the following pages two essays on the rule of law in Germany, a nation where the degeneration of that rule into arbitrary government was the most obvious, and which is now faced by serious problems of law and order. Influenced by Dicey, these essays emphasize the need of freedom from the government, as well as the necessity of authority for the sake of freedom, by showing the relationship between two German versions of the rule of law, namely, *Rechtsstaat* and *Staatsrecht*.

These terms are difficult to translate, and one is tempted not to translate them at all. Literal translations simply would be "Law State" and "State Law," respectively. In these composite words, "state" means any kind of state, such as Germany, Bavaria, Prussia, or Saxony, and not just, as it often does in American usage,

[9] *Ibid.*, 188.

a member-state of a federation. Rendering "Recht" by "law" is justified in view of the fact that "law" can include older, natural, and customary law, as well as any kind of written law, and also comprises right and justice. However, the words "Law State" and "State Law" sound a bit awkward. And whereas a point could be made for using these literal translations to be exact, they will be avoided whenever their replacement does not jeopardize meaning. The term "Rechtsstaat" was coined in the beginning of German constitutionalism, early in the nineteenth century. It basically denotes constitutionalism or constitutional government and therefore will often be replaced by these terms. *Staatsrecht* is the law concerned with the organization of a state and its government, and the relationship between the individual and the public power. In German public law, it is distinguished from administrative law, criminal law, and tax law. Aside from this narrow concept of State Law, there can be said to exist a wider concept, meaning the total legal framework of any given society, or state. Since *Recht* implies justice, the term "Rechtsstaat" will also be translated "Just State." And since State Law provides for the kind of justice that exists under that law in any particular state, the word "Staatsrecht" will also be translated "State Justice."

The first chapter, "Rechtsstaat and Staatsrecht," or "The Just State and State Justice," was written in 1966, when threats to the rule of law generally were believed to come from big government. It shows how specific State Law determined the concept of justice prevailing in any particular state, making it a national, social, even a national-socialist Law State, and demon-

6

strates how these types of "Law States" came to threaten classic constitutionalism.

The second chapter, "Staatsrecht and Rechtsstaat," or "State Justice and the Just State," written five years later—years characterized by permissiveness and a decline of law and order—emphasizes that the friends of constitutional government, in spite of the justified fear of big government, should not forget that constitutionalism, or the Just State, is not possible without law and law enforcement, and that it is endangered as much by government impotence as by government omnipotence.

I

THE JUST STATE
AND
STATE JUSTICE

LINGUISTICALLY, "Staatsrecht" appears to be an inversion of "Rechtsstaat." From the point of view of content, things are not much different: the Law State came into existence as a reaction to the State Law of the police state and was later distorted by the State Law. *Nomen est omen.*

I

It has been said that, as distinguished from the French, the Germans are unable to think in clear concepts.[1] From the Anglo-Saxon world, they appear in a different light. They are credited with the gift of coining clear formal concepts for what in the Anglo-Saxon countries remains vague material substance. For instance, even in the mother country of modern federalism there have so far not come into existence terms corresponding to *Staatenbund* and *Bundesstaat,* in spite

[1] Carl Schmitt, *Politische Romantik* (2d ed. 1925) 3.

9

of the fact that the cruel Civil War in large measure took place because people could not agree as to how "federal" was to be interpreted.[2]

The situation is similar in the case of the "rule of law." True, that rule is usually distinguished from the "rule of men." [3] However, since the rule of law is a rule of men, in so far as in the last analysis it is determined by men, it approaches the "rule of men" quite closely. This possibility is inherent in the term "rule of law," for that term is ambiguous. It may mean the rule of the best law which stands above the ruler and is respected by him, as well as the rule of the worst law which is arbitrarily made and executed by a tyrant. It all depends on how "rule" and "law" are understood and what is emphasized. Aside from the fact that "law" may mean justice, right, as well as statute, "rule of law" may have different meanings in so far as emphasis may be put upon "rule" or "law." "Rule," probably used because Harrington spoke of the "empire of laws, and not of men," [4] means, as distinguished from "reign," an actual rule which can be determined by men only. Thus, the more emphasis is put upon "rule" in the expression "rule of law," the more we are probably confronted with empire, state, power, government, regimentation, and the less

[2] Comp. Alpheus T. Mason, "The Nature of Our Federal Union Reconsidered," *Political Science Quarterly* LXV (1950) 502. The ambiguity about the meaning of the words "federal," "confederate," "confederation," "confederacy" is already evident the the classic commentary to the American Constitution, *The Federalist*. See the author's *The Federalist* (1960) 125, 154.

[3] The origin of the rule of law and its various interpretations in various countries is described in Friedrich A. Hayek, *The Constitution of Liberty* (1960) 162 ff., 176 ff., 193 ff. The rule of law became best known through A. V. Dicey's *Introduction to the Study of the Law of the Constitution*.

[4] James Harrington, *Oceana* (1656, 1887) 16.

with law. So much regimentation can exist that even the best law will hardly be evident, especially if law means statute and not right or justice. The "rule of law" thus can approach the "rule of men" quite closely, just as the latter can be a demonstration of law in the sense of right and justice rather than in that of regimentation. Although this has been recognized in the Anglo-Saxon world,[5] and although many definitions of the "rule of law" have come about, no terms which would clearly distinguish the major variations of that rule have been developed.

In my opinion, such terms are present in the German words "Rechtsstaat" and "Staatsrecht." These words connect what is naturally connected, law and state,[6] and yet show that this connection can exist in different ways, in favor of the law or the state. Although in a Law State there can exist different degrees of law and state, the former will always have primacy before the latter, as indicated by the—symbolic—word "Law State." And although the State Law can harbor different degrees of state and law, the state and its concept of justice will always come before the law and its more abstract notion of justice. The objection may be made that the Law State and State Law belong to different categories which cannot be compared; that the Law State, as the Just State, can at best be distinguished from the unjust state, or from the power-state; and State

[5] For instance, Harry W. Jones, "The Rule of Law and the Welfare State," *Columbia Law Review* LVIII (1958) 143 ff.; Sir Ivor Jennings, *The Law and the Constitution* (5th ed. 1959) 42 ff.

[6] As to the relationship of law and state, comp. Otto Gierke, *Deutsches Privatrecht* I (1895) 112 ff., *Althusius und die Entwicklung der naturrechtlichen Staatstheorien* (3rd ed. 1913) 264 ff.; Richard Thoma, "Rechtsstaatsidee und Verwaltungsrechtswissenschaft," *Jahrbuch des öffentlichen Rechts* IV (1910) 201–204.

Law, from such species of law as private law or criminal law. This indeed is a common, not at all "senseless"[7] opinion. Nevertheless, it is perhaps an all too simple way of thinking. For the Just State probably is challenged as little merely by the unjust state as justice is by injustice. Things are more complicated.

The struggle for the law is not merely concerned with justice and injustice as absolute values and the distance between them, but also with their respective scope and their proximity. It is concerned with their interlocking, with the fact that injustice produces justice, and justice, injustice. Without injustice no justice, without justice no injustice. It is the connection and interdependence of justice and injustice which always shifts the borderline between the two, decreases the immunity of the one from the other, lets justice prevail over, or succumb to, injustice.[8] Only the layman asks crudely for justice and injustice, and not every layman is content with that. All is a matter of the degree of justice and injustice. Lawmaking does not mean making general norms, to the effect that, for instance, larceny is punished by a prison term of three months, but to the effect that it is punished by a term ranging from one day to five years. Furthermore, lawmaking means to determine that

[7] Carl Schmitt, "Was bedeutet der Streit um den 'Rechtsstaat'?", *Zeitschrift für die gesamte Staatswissenschaft* XCV (1935) 189, criticizes: "*Rechtsstaat* was said to be the opposite of *Non-Rechtsstaat in the sense of the unjust state* (power-state, force-state, arbitrary state, police state), which of course makes it easy to let the Rechtsstaat triumph over such an adversary. But things are not that simple in the great spiritual struggles of peoples and time. Here sense does not struggle with nonsense, but with counter-sense, and life with life."

[8] A compilation of different definitions of "law" and arguments that such definitions are worthless can be found in William Seagle, *The History of Law* (1946) 3 ff.

grand and petty larceny are punished more severely or more leniently. Similarly, to adjudicate means to judge the illegal act according to law, means measuring each particular case. Church robbers and thieves of food are sentenced individually, and not summarily, and their degree of punishment may differ. The closeness of justice and injustice rather than the distance between them creates the problems which lead us into the juristic twilight without which we cannot find the light.

The situation is similar with respect to the relationship between the Just State and the unjust state. To understand the former state, we must not contrast it to the latter. This would secure for it too easy a victory. We must weigh the Just State with something that is more closely related to it than the unjust state. We must look for a concept whose elements are similar to those of the Just State, a concept that can have a more fertilizing effect upon it than the unjust state. Such a concept is State Law. Although generally it will be the law set by the state, it can also be the law guarded by the state, just as Law State, generally understood to be a state which guards the law, can also be a state that makes law.[9] In State Law, law and state are as close as in Law State. Thus a fruitful comparison appears to be possible. Everything becomes a matter of emphasis upon the components. For if, in view of their identical components, the use of different words such as "Law State" and "State Law" makes sense, then the relative weight of the two components in each word must be a different one. We want to examine what this relative weight has been and ask whether a shift in weight in

[9] See *infra,* note 57.

favor of the state has made the law suffer, whether State Justice has restricted the Just State.

This possibility exists, especially in view of the facts that the law of a state may prescribe and has prescribed a Law State, and that the latter can flourish and has flourished because of that fact. The mutual replacement of related, or, at least, compatible values is more probable than that of opposed and incompatible values, especially if it occurs gradually and inconspicuously. Changes then more easily appear to be legitimate and no cause for concern. Thus as a rule, a gradual restriction of states' rights, brought about under assurances that the federal structure of the nation would prevail, will be more easily effected than a sudden abolition of those rights, especially if it is accompanied by the admission that a unitary state will be established. A gradual restriction of judicial and legislative powers will be permitted if it is stressed that the principles of the separation of powers will be preserved. A sudden abolition of those powers, on the other hand, will meet with considerable resistance, especially if the intention to concentrate all power in the executive is not concealed. Restrictions of property rights will be more easily attained if they are brought about gradually with the assurance that, in principle, property will remain protected than if they are made suddenly under threats of totally abolishing such property. Since welfare legislation appears to be more harmless than a communist revolution, it is, as far as the protection of property in the long run is concerned, perhaps more dangerous.[10]

[10] Comp. the author's *In Defense of Property* (1963) 124 ff., 183 ff., 241, note 126. The risks of evolution are also pointed out in my "Will the Presidency Incite Assassination?" *Ethics* LXXVI (1965) 14 ff.

The case is not different with restrictions of the Just State. They can easily be brought about under a State Law which claims to be oriented toward that state. They will be more difficult to achieve suddenly under a law which is openly opposed to justice. We are afraid that German law has harmed justice not only when openly opposing it, but, less obviously though perhaps more remarkably, also when professing allegiance to it. In the following, the question of the existence of constitutionalism in Germany will be examined.

That question has often been asked. It seems that every generation has tried to adorn an existing or desired State Law with the attributes of justice and to emphasize that such law corresponded to the Just State, possibly to an improved or refined version. In that endeavor, the Just State was usually pitted against the unjust state or the power-state.[11] Carl Schmitt, who questioned the meaning of the Law State in 1934, who opposed the "principle of the Law State, 'nulla poena sine lege,' to the principle of justice, 'nullum crimen sine poena,'"[12] and stressed "the immediate justice of the sentence *nullum crimen sine poena,*"[13] took a different course. He did not pit the Law State against the unjust state, nor was he particularly in favor of the former. This probably was no longer advantageous to him. We are not motivated by opportunism when we agree with Schmitt in many ways.[14] We want the Just State, but are skeptical as to its future. And we shall not pit it against

[11] Comp. Hermann Heller, *Rechtsstaat oder Diktatur?* (1930) and Friedrich Darmstaedter, *Rechtsstaat oder Machtstaat* (1932).

[12] Schmitt, "Nationalsozialismus und Rechtsstaat," *Juristische Wochenschrift* LXIII (1934) 714.

[13] "Was bedeutet der Streit um den 'Rechtsstaat'?" 196.

[14] Comp. Hayek, *Constitution of Liberty* 485.

the unjust state, but measure it by State Law. Our ex-
amination seems to be proper a generation after the
publication of Schmitt's contribution. For in the mean-
time there has passed not only the national-socialist
epoch, but also an even longer period of the social Law
State under the Bonn Basic Law.

II

The Law State came about as a reaction against the
State Law, without, however, being able to emancipate
itself totally from it.

The Law State has been considered "the opposite of
two kinds of state, namely, the Christian state, i.e., a
state determined by religion, and the moral state, i.e.,
the state of Prussian officialdom as described in the
political philosophy of Hegel." Its origin has been derived from "the historical situation of the German 19th
century." [15] This contains part of, but not the whole,
truth. Law is not as much opposed to religion and
morals as has been indicated in the preceding passage,
although there are, of course, tensions among those concepts. Truly enough, constitutionalism was a reaction
against Prussian officialdom and its state. But it was
such a reaction not so much because that state was a
moral one, but because it was a policed one—a police
state. Similarly, the Law State came into existence as a
reaction against a state determined by religion only in
so far as the latter had the idea of the divine right of
kings written on its banners and presented itself as a

[15] Schmitt, "Was bedeutet der Streit um den 'Rechtsstaat'?" 191.
Comp. also "Nationalsozialismus und Rechtsstaat" 714.

police state. Constitutionalism is not a reaction against a state which is determined by religion in so far as its rejection of the divine right of kings is based upon divine law. What, finally, concerns the assertion that constitutional government can be explained from the historical situation in nineteenth-century Germany, that assertion is correct only if one understands that situation by taking into account intellectual currents coming to Germany from the West. Among those currents, the most important of which originated with Locke, Montesquieu, Rousseau, and Burke, the idea of the "empire of laws, not of men," as it had developed mainly in England and America,[16] played an important role. That idea was, to use an expression of Oliver Wendell Holmes, "a brooding omnipresence in the sky."[17]

Of great importance were the writings of Kant, which have often been considered the source of the discussion about constitutional government.[18] It has also been pointed out that it probably was not accidental that the movement leading to the development of the idea of that type of government began in Hanover, which

[16] For the opinion that the American Revolution was based upon Whig ideas, comp. Edmund Burke, *Speech on Conciliation with America* (1775); Otto Vossler, *Die amerikanischen Revolutionsideale in ihrem Verhältnis zu den europäischen* (1929); Charles H. McIlwain, *The American Revolution* (1923) 156 ff., 183 ff. Chief Justice Marshall stated: "The government of the United States has been emphatically termed a government of laws, and not of men." Marbury v. Madison, 5 U. S. (1 Cranch) 137, 163 (1803).

[17] However, Holmes emphasized that the common law was "not a brooding omnipresence in the sky but the articulate voice of some sovereign or quasi-sovereign that can be identified." Southern Pacific Co. v. Jansen, 244 U. S. 205, 222 (1917).

[18] Hayek, *Constitution of Liberty* 196 f. Schmitt, "Nationalsozialismus und Rechtsstaat" 714, refers to Kant as the "philosopher of the 'Rechtsstaat'." Comp. also Werner Haensel, *Kants Lehre vom Widerstandsrecht* (1930).

17

through its monarchs had more contact with England than other German states. There scholars like Brandes, Rehberg, Dahlmann, and von Berg, who were influenced by the ideas of the Whigs, tried to spread the idea of the rule of law throughout Germany.[19] It is probably also not just coincidental that Robert von Mohl, who has been considered the father of the Law State,[20] and probably contributed more to the spread of that concept than any other man, was a student of American government.[21]

In the beginning of the nineteenth century, people saw in the writings of Kant a polemic against the police state and an advocacy of the rights of the individual. Kant saw the purpose of the state not in the happiness

[19] Hayek, *Constitution of Liberty* 482. Comp. Hermann Christern, *Deutscher Ständestaat und englischer Parlamentarismus am Ende des 18. Jahrhunderts* (1939) 149 ff., 172 ff., 202 ff., 217 ff.; Gustav Marchet, *Studien über die Entwicklung der Verwaltungslehre in Deutschland* (1885) 421 ff.

[20] Comp. Lorenz von Stein, *Die Verwaltungslehre* I, 1 (2d ed. 1869) 297; Rudolf Gneist, *Der Rechtsstaat* (1872) 184; Richard Thoma, "Rechtsstaatsidee" 197. Erich Angermann, *Robert von Mohl* (1962) 116, shows that Mohl found the term "Rechtsstaat" already in existence. This work also contains a discussion of Mohl's concept of the Rechtsstaat. Mohl himself described the history of constitutionalism since the Middle Ages in *Die Geschichte und Literatur der Staatswissenschaften* I (1855) 227 ff.

[21] Mohl perhaps was the German authority on the American Constitution in the first half of the nineteenth century. His *Das Bundes-Staatsrecht der Vereinigten Staaten von Nord-Amerika* was published in 1824. His review of Joseph Story's *Commentaries on the Constitution of the United States*, "Nordamerikanisches Staatsrecht," *Kritische Zeitschrift für Rechtswissenschaft und Gesetzgebung des Auslandes* VII (1835) 1 ff., impressed so favorably that it was translated in *American Jurist* XIV (1835) 330 ff. and XV (1836) 1 ff. In his later years, Mohl also wrote on American developments. See the author's "Robert von Mohl, Germany's de Tocqueville," in Dietze, ed., *Essays on the American Constitution A Commemorative Volume in Honor of Alpheus T. Mason* (1964) 187 ff.

and welfare (*Glückseligkeit, Wohlfahrt*) [22]—the police in a broader sense—but in "the greatest harmony of the constitution with the principles of law (*Rechtsprinzipien*) . . . , which reason orders us to strive for by a categorical imperative," i.e., in the securing of "legal freedom." [23] The Hanoverian scholars mentioned above used similar arguments in their attempts to constitutionalize the police power for the sake of the freedom of the individual. [24]

It is not much different with Mohl, upon whom we shall dwell a little longer because of his far-reaching influence. Thoma touches an important point when he remarks that it was no mere coincidence that Mohl, the scholar who first divided State Law into constitutional and administrative law, also introduced the concept of the Law State into the science of law. [25] It is indeed of importance that Mohl divided the positive State Law and thus weakened it, and with it, the power of the state. Mohl opposed State Law that was oriented toward the police state, and his concept of the Just State derived from this attitude. To Mohl, that state was a constitutional government which weakened, and perhaps replaced, the law of the police state. Reason of

[22] Immanuel Kant, *Rechtslehre*, in *Gesammelte Schriften* (ed. by the Prussian Academy of Sciences), Sec. 1, VI (1911) 318; "Über den Gemeinspruch: Das mag in der Theorie richtig sein, taugt aber nicht für die Praxis," *ibid.* VIII (1912) 289 f., 298.

[23] *Rechtslehre* 318, 314; "Gemeinspruch" 298. Comp. Angermann, *Robert von Mohl* 109.

[24] Christern, *Deutscher Ständestaat;* Marchet, *Entwicklung der Verwaltungslehre.*

[25] "Rechtsstaatsidee" 197. Mohl's distinction between constitutional and administrative law can already be found in his *Bundes-Staatsrecht der Vereinigten Staaten von Nord-Amerika.*

state was replaced by a "rational" state (*Verstandes-Staat*) for which Mohl, after some hesitation, chose the term "Rechtsstaat." [26] This state was to determine the law of the community. Law and justice were given priority over the state.

In a book on the State Law of Württemberg (which was published after his study on the constitution of the United States), Mohl stressed the rational activity of the police according to law. In his major work on the police-science according to the principles of the Law State (1832), he elaborated that idea. The title is revealing. The idea of the police state is fading away. Mohl no longer speaks of the police, but of "police-science" according to the principles of constitutionalism. The police no longer appears as something arbitrary, but as something reasonable and scientific. It acts according to a rational law, a law which is characteristic of the Just State. This state is for Mohl not, as has been asserted, "merely . . . the rational state, irrespective of whether it appears in the form of the absolute or constitutional state," [27] but only a constitutional state which came about as a reaction against the police state.[28] Mohl conceived that state to be something substantive and material, not merely something procedural and formal. It reflected not so much the possibly arbitrary and emotional policy of the ruler, but that constitutional and scientific policy which had been advocated for the protection of the rights of the individual from arbitrary government by the classic representatives of modern

[26] *Das Staatsrecht des Königreiches Württemberg* I (1829) 11, note 3.
[27] Thoma, "Rechtsstaatsidee" 197 f.
[28] Similarly Schmitt, "Was bedeutet der Streit um den 'Rechtstaat'?" 190.

constitutional government, such as Locke, Montesquieu, and the authors of *The Federalist*.[29] The primary justification for the Law State was individualism. It had the "tendency of limiting the activities of the state to the most necessary functions. It is, in a word, in tune with the constitutional and economic ideas of the older liberalism."[30] Constitutional government primarily was a "reaction against infringements by the police state."[31]

The fact that constitutionalism came into being as a reaction to the police state does not mean, however, that it was absolutely opposed to all police. The new

[29] Without doubt Mohl has been influenced by these representatives of constitutionalism. He wrote about them. *Die Geschichte und Literatur der Staatswissenschaften* I (1855) 24 ff., 190, 230 ff., 236 f., 249 ff.; III (1858) 386 f. Montesquieu the political scientist is discussed in Franz Neumann's introduction to *The Spirit of the Laws* (1949) xxix ff.; in Emile Durkheim's dissertation on Montesquieu's contribution to social sciences (1892), in *Montesquieu and Rousseau* (1960) 1 ff; in Georges Davy, "Durkheim, Montesquieu, and Rousseau," *ibid.*, 144 ff.; in Louis Althusser, *Montesquieu* (1964) 5 ff.; in Sergio Cotta, *Montesquieu e la scienza della società* (1953). *The Federalist*, which reflects the ideas of Locke and Montesquieu, emphasizes the value of political science for the freedom of the individual. In essay 9, Hamilton lauds the "science of politics" and its achievements. In essay 37, Madison speaks in a similar way of the "science of government" and "political science," and in essay 43 he praises Montesquieu as the advocate of the separation of powers, "this invaluable precept in the science of politics." Mohl the political scientist is mentioned in Carl J. Friedrich, *Der Verfassungsstaat der Neuzeit* (1953) vii.

[30] Thoma, "Rechtsstaatsidee" 198. Comp. Mohl, *Die Polizei-Wissenschaft nach den Grundsätzen des Rechtsstaates* I (1832) 7, 14: "The freedom of the citizen is . . . the supreme principle . . . , therefore, the support of the state can only be something negative and only consist in the removal of obstacles which the individual would be unable to remove all by himself. . . . The whole state only has the function to protect and make possible freedom."

[31] Thoma, *op. cit.* 198. Schmitt's criticism, "that the crude slogan Law State contra police state was indoctrinated as a 'juristic' and strictly 'scientific' distinction as 'ruling' dogma to German law students and young officials for a whole generation" ("Was bedeutet der Streit um den 'Rechtsstaat'?" 191), confirms this fact.

21

remains the captive of the old. If revolutionary movements do not effect an absolute break with the past, evolutionary movements can be expected to do so even less. The movement for the Just State remained a captive of the law of the police state. It was thus, in a way, schizophrenic. True, Kant's idea that the function of the state was restricted to a realization of the idea of the law (*Rechtsidee*) continued to have some popularity.[32] However, it did not remain representative of general public opinion. Its influences waned after it was felt in the first decades of the nineteenth century that the worst abuses of the police state had been overcome. Kant's ideas made room for a school of thought which no longer saw the task of the state exclusively in the realization of the law, but also in the pursuit of welfare policy. Although this school rejected an arbitrary police, it did not object to a "good police," provided such a police acted in the manner prescribed by law. Mohl never was much opposed to that school. As time passed, he moved closer and closer to it. Whereas in the beginning he had favored the term "Law State" over *"rational state"* (and probably not, as has been asserted, merely for want of a better, more current term),[33] and had left no doubt about the material content of the Just State, he nevertheless deviated from

[32] Wilhelm Joseph Behr has been considered a "prototypical representative of that school." Angermann, *Robert von Mohl* 124. Comp. his *System der angewandten allgemeinen Staatslehre oder der Staatskunst (Politik)* (1810), and *Allgemeine Polizei-Wissenschaftslehre oder Pragmatische Theorie der Polizei-Gesetzgebung und Verwaltung. Zur Ehrenrettung rechtsgemässer Polizei, mittelst scharfer Zeichnung ihrer wahren Sphäre und Grenzen* (1848).

[33] Angermann, *op. cit.* 131, writes that Mohl "adopted the name 'Rechtsstaat' . . . only for want of a—current—better name." It is true that Mohl wrote that he felt the term was "not quite fitting in so

22

the Kantian ideal by permitting more leeway to the police.[34] Later on, Mohl's deviation from Kant became even more obvious. He appeared less individualistic, and more in sympathy with concerns of the group, society and the state,[35] although he never really repudiated the ideas of his early manhood.[36] Also, Mohl in his

---

far as *Law* constitutes only one half of this species of state; it should be called 'law- and police state', to be exact. Perhaps best of all *reason-state?" Das Staatsrecht des Königreiches Württemberg* I, 11, note 3. In my opinion Mohl decided to use the term "Rechtsstaat," after carefully weighing the merits of the other terms, because he wanted, above all, to emphasize the primacy of the law.

[34] Comp. Angermann, *op. cit.* 107 ff.

[35] In the first edition of his *Polizeiwissenschaft* (1832), Mohl wrote: "A Rechtsstaat can have one purpose only: to order the people's living together in such a way as to support and promote every member of society in the freest and most comprehensive possible use of all his abilities" (I, 7). In the second edition of 1844, he remarked that "by no means has the state the task of pursuing different individual purposes (*verschiedene Einzelzwecke*), because this would be absolutely impossible. However, it has the purpose of realizing the total interest (*Gesamt-Lebensansicht*) of the people" (I, 7, note 1). In the third edition of 1866 Mohl wrote, "a little more cautiously" (Angermann, *op. cit.* 122), that the state naturally does not assume the role of "an assistant to every citizen" (I, 12), but creates general "establishments and institutions which benefit all those who want to move in a certain direction." "It is, furthermore, a wrong assumption that the life-purposes (*Lebenszwecke*) of the individuals are quite different and constitute an atomistic and unmanageable mass" (I, 13). "We only request that the state with its enormous power not only refrain from interfering with the realization of a people's specific life-purposes, but that it promote such realization as far as possible" (I, 15). Mohl speaks of the "wrong basic idea that the state is exclusively an institution for the protection of the law" (I, 16). Comp. Angermann, *op. cit.* 119 ff.

[36] In 1841, Mohl wrote: ". . . the individual keeps himself distinct and independent. He wants to find his own satisfaction, to educate himself according to his means and inclinations, and does not at all consider it desirable to be absorbed by the whole, and to perfect the life of the community (*und keineswegs erachtet es das Aufgehen im Ganzen, die vollendete Darstellung der Gesamtheit, als seine Aufgabe*). Everything is well with the community only in so far as all individuals attain their similar aims; community life is only to promote

23

later years stressed the formal aspect of constitutionalism at the cost of the material one.[37] The idea gained ground that the right state must not only be a state which restricts state activity to a minimum, but could also be a state that could curtail the rights of the in-

the purposes of individuals, and not vice versa. Therefore, nobody must be put at the disposal of the whole as a mere means or even be sacrificed to it. Perhaps there are more beautiful ideals of living together. On the other hand there probably never existed a people which would have succeeded in developing morally in a community (*Gesamtheit*) which promised the realization of these ideals. The egoistic and atomistic view of life and state has at least the advantage of preventing the crippling of all individuals by a wrongly conceived aim of the community." "Polizei," in Carl von Rotteck and Carl Welcker, *Staats-Lexikon oder Enzyklopädie der Staatswissenschaften* XII 644. In 1859, Mohl wrote in *Encyklopädie der Staatswissenschaften* 101, 325, that "the purpose and usefulness of the state does not consist in a wholesome community life, but in the immediate satisfaction of the individuals and of special groups of the society. The individual is as little absorbed by the whole as the human being by the citizen. Quite to the contrary: the state expands and restricts its services according to the reasonable requests of the individual, and the individual is a citizen only for the purpose of attaining his human aims." "Isolation thus remains the rule; the social group, on the other hand, is nothing but a complement to isolation out of necessity. The same applies on a higher level to the state." In 1866 he wrote: "It cannot be admitted that the state should take into consideration the wants of society only, and not those of the individual. While the organic act of entering a community creates wants of that community which naturally deserve attention, the individuality of the individual does by no means cease to be justified within the group to which it belongs. Every individual human existence must be developed and satisfied in its individuality. Otherwise there would be no reasonable explanation for life on earth. To limit state welfare to the community means to misunderstand the character of the modern Rechtsstaat completely. . . ." These and similar statements can be found together with the remarks mentioned in note 35, remarks that indicate a sympathy for the interests of society, in the third edition of his *Polizeiwissenschaft* I, 14. It is interesting to note that here Mohl also takes issue with Stahl because the latter "assigns to the state only the welfare of society in so far as the state is supposed to take over the role of God in the leadership of the community, but not in the leadership of the individuals. . . ."

[37] Angermann, *Robert von Mohl* 113 f.

dividual as long as this was done under the procedures prescribed by law.

Thus constitutionalism remained a captive of the police even with its most ardent advocate. It remained a captive of law made by the leaders of the state. It remained a captive of the state's law. Although the Law State had been conceived as a reaction against the police state, and although it put law and justice above the state, it did not secure the continuance of this condition. It made no provision to prevent the state from again elevating its will over the just law, something that could easily occur in view of the concessions that had been made to the so-called "good police" even by the founders of constitutional government. For on the basis of these concessions that government had to be in tune with every program of "good police," i.e., with every program that was considered good by those who held power provided it was carried out in prescribed forms. This means that practically every governmental program would be in conformity with the Law State. This emphasis was likely to bring about a return from the importance of the law to that of the state and, potentially, from the "good" to the "bad" police. For as soon as everything which the law of the state prescribed could pass as "good police," the difference between good and bad police was likely to become blurred. Under the cloak of good police, everything could become bad police. *Summum ius summa iniuria.*

III

Whereas originally constitutionalism determined the law of the state, it was later reoriented by that law.

Mohl had left open the possibility of a merely formal concept of constitutional government. His contemporary Stahl left no doubt about it: "The state must be a Law State, this is the catchword and truly also the moving power of the time. It must exactly determine and definitely secure the scope and limits of its activity and the free sphere of its citizens according to the law, and must realize moral ideas directly only in so far as it is absolutely necessary. This is the concept of the Law State. It means that the state is not merely concerned with the legal order without any administrative purposes, or that it is concerned only with the protection of the rights of the individual. Constitutionalism is not at all concerned with the purpose and content of the state, but only with the manner and character of realizing them." [38] Since this definition of the Law State is considered classic,[39] we shall examine it a little more closely.

Most obvious in it is that the material concept of constitutional government is replaced by a formal one.

[38] Friedrich Julius Stahl, *Philosophie des Rechts* II, part 2 (3rd ed. 1856) 137 f. Stahl continues: "The Rechtsstaat is thus distinguished, above all, from the *patriarchal*, the *patrimonial*, and the sheer *police* state, in which the government tries to realize moral ideas and useful ends in their totality after a moral, and thus arbitrary, appreciation of each particular case. The Rechtsstaat must, however, be as much distinguished from the *popular state* (Rousseau, Robespierre), . . . in which the people think that every citizen possesses a complete and positive political virtue on account of the state, and that their own standard of morals is not restricted by any legal barrier. The condition mentioned first is a natural beginning which must be overcome, whereas the condition mentioned last is an absolute aberration of judgment."

[39] Otto Bähr put this definition at the beginning of his *Der Rechtsstaat* (1864). Rudolf Gneist, *Der Rechtsstaat* (1872) 16, remarks: "What Stahl calls 'Rechtsstaat' found the general agreement of all his opponents." Comp. also Thoma, "Rechtsstaatsidee" 198, 201.

It has, correctly, been called "the definition of the formal Law State." [40] But it is probably more than that. It also says something about the material substance of that state. After confessing his faith in constitutional government, Stahl requests that by means of law that government exactly determine and definitely secure the scope and limits of its activity and the free sphere of its citizens. The sequence is significant. The "scope" precedes the "limits" of state activity, and that activity precedes the "free sphere" of the citizens. The words "exactly determine" precede the words "definitely securing." Stahl, who has been called a "strangely inconsequent thinker," [41] here appears to be quite consequent: he clearly denounces the liberal Law State, a state in which the rights of the citizen are basically unrestricted and the power of the government is basically limited. It could be argued that the remark that the Law State must realize and enforce moral ideas only in so far as they belong to the sphere of law and as is absolutely necessary, is expressive of liberal ideas. However, this remark hardly is a match for what is stated before and after it. Furthermore, it could be interpreted in a way that makes it harmonize with the rest of the definition: we need only understand under "law" a law that has been made by the state legislator—a statute.

At any rate, there can be little doubt that Stahl's concept of the Law State is quite different from Mohl's. Mohl's concept is primarily a material one, and only secondarily a formal one. Stahl's, on the other hand, is

---

[40] *Ibid.* 201.
[41] *Ibid.* 198. Thoma admits, however, that Stahl distinguished between the purpose of the state and the form to realize those purposes. This is evident in the sentences quoted in note 38.

primarily formal and, at best, secondarily material. Whereas Mohl puts the rights of the individual before the might of the state, it is the other way around with Stahl. Mohl, who derived his concept of the Just State from a polemic against the law of the police state and yet remained a captive of that law, put the Law State before the State Law. Stahl, who derived his concept of the Law State from a polemic against the liberal state and yet was a captive of a law that existed prior to the state and was determined by religion, subordinated the Law State to the State Law and made the former a mere facade for the latter. Thus constitutional government, as far as its material content is concerned, could mean everything, could be used and abused for anything. It could become a mere "means," a mere "method," a "neutral" apparatus [42] for the execution of any kind of law, even if such law were detrimental to law and justice. Constitutionalism could be determined and reoriented by the positive law of the state in any way. During the Third Reich, this led, without much ado, to its annihilation. Because of its prestige—which with increasing formalization became less and less warranted—the formal Law State was likely to hide the danger which State Law constituted to law and justice. Mohl is perhaps as responsible for this development as Stahl, for he did not sufficiently provide for the protection of constitutionalism from state activity. Flirting with the "good police," he left a breach which could be widened by the enemies of the original, genuine, liberal Just State.

There is, of course, a long way from Mohl's ideal to

[42] Schmitt, "Was bedeutet der Streit um den 'Rechtsstaat'?" 193 f.

Hitler's authoritarian power state. But this road was smoother than one would imagine. For it was smoothed by a written State Law which, as it became captivated by nationalism, statism, and socialism, more and more renounced liberal ideas. Thus the decline of constitutional government can be said to have started with Stahl's Christian Law State and to have been completed with the *Weltanschauungsstaat* of national socialism. The stages in between show the decline of constitutionalism through its formalization and de-liberalization.

For some time after its conception, the Law State was very popular. Stahl's remark that it was the catchword and the driving force [43] of the time was a truism. It appeared to be a mirror of existing law.[44] The term was much in use. In 1864 Otto Bähr published *Der Rechtsstaat;* eight years later, Rudolf Gneist produced a book with the same title. In 1878 Maurus published a book on the modern Law State as a constitutional state, and a year later there appeared Lorenz von Stein's "Rechtsstaat und Verwaltungsrechtspflege." [45] In the same year, the second edition of Gneist's work on the Law State and administrative courts in Germany came out.

[43] Stahl's use of the word "Entwicklungstrieb" is perhaps telling because this word indicates emotional political passion, as distinguished from rational political science. Perhaps Stahl envisaged the future development, in which many different substances were poured into the form of the Law State. Perhaps this word sneaked into Stahl's definition by a dispensation of providence at a time when the original Just State, oriented toward the individual, was beginning to be determined by the existing government.

[44] Comp. Gneist, *Der Rechtsstaat*, foreword.

[45] *Grünhuts Zeitschrift für das private und öffentliche Recht der Gegenwart* VI (1879) 27 ff.; see also his *Die vollziehende Gewalt* I (2d ed. 1869) 296 ff.

However, with a few exceptions,[46] all of these authors believed in the formal concept of constitutionalism. Thus it was chiefly that concept which was fashionable. The Law State was something which, since it was barren of a material content, was an "empty shell of legality," [47] a vacuum which needed to be filled with some substance. This substance could, of course, be a liberal one, which would subordinate itself to the normativism of the formal concept of constitutional government.[48] Potentially, it could be a substance that would distort and destroy the material essence of that government and make a farce even out of the latter's formal ingredients.[49] Thus, due to its formalization, constitutionalism was at the mercy of the best and worst legis-

[46] Maurus, for instance, proceeds from a law that can be found by reason. Positive laws that are incompatible with that law are unjust. "In a *Just State*, legislation and administration must be ordered according to justice (*Recht*), and all infringements by the state upon the freedom of the citizens must be in conformity with 'justice' (*Recht*)." "The state . . . in which injustice legally exists or can exist, is not the Just State." Heinrich Maurus, *Der moderne Verfassungsstaat als Rechtsstaat* (1878) 59, 110.

[47] Ulrich Scheuner, "Die neuere Entwicklung des Rechtsstaats in Deutschland," *Hundert Jahre Deutsches Rechtsleben. Eine Festschrift zum hundertjährigen Bestehen des Deutschen Juristentages 1860–1960* II (1960) 248.

[48] Schmitt, "Was bedeutet der Streit um den 'Rechtsstaat'?" 194. Schmitt seems to share my opinion, although he writes that "this 'formal' concept no longer has any content, but can have any content." The formal Law State has, of course, a content. The question is whether this content constitutes a material equivalent to the formal concept, i.e., whether its substance guarantees what the formal Law State is supposed to guarantee, namely, the protection of the individual from arbitrary government. Experience has shown that this often was not the case. Where the proper substance is missing, proper forms are of little avail.

[49] The dangers of a formalization of constitutional government are shown by Werner Kaegi, "Rechtsstaat und Demokratie," in *Demokratie und Rechtsstaat, Festgabe für Giacometti* (1953) 132 ff. Comp. Angermann, *Robert von Mohl* 191 ff.

lation which could determine it in any way. Although the law of the state, by providing the formal Law State with a material content, could demonstrate its inclination toward the Just State, it could also deform and erode that state. It is thus not surprising that at the time of the popularity of the mere formal Law State, State Law gained ground,[50] whereas genuine constitutionalism began to fade, until it disappeared during the Third Reich.

In the beginning, it is true, constitutionalism showed itself to be rather viable, for its friends left no doubt about its liberal content. Thus in the early 1860s, Lasker clearly distinguished it from the police state and without reservation expressed himself in its favor.[51] Five years later, Jacoby emphasized its superiority to the national state. Stressing that he was fighting for the "Just and Constitutional State," he requested Bismarck's dismissal and said of the victories of the Prussian army that they were neither "a credit to the Prussian people, nor a blessing to the whole German fatherland."[52] The efforts of German liberals were not without success. They became transmuted into law.[53]

[50] Comp. Hermann Rehm, *Geschichte der Staatsrechtswissenschaft* (1896) 260 ff.

[51] Eduard Lasker, "Polizeigewalt und Rechtsschutz in Preussen," *Deutsche Jahrbücher für Politik und Literatur* I (1861), esp. 44 ff.

[52] Speech of Aug. 23, 1866. *Stenographische Berichte* I (1866) 73.

[53] Comp. Georg Jellinek, *Allgemeine Staatslehre* (2d ed. 1905) 353, 768 ff.; Richard Schmidt, *Allgemeine Staatslehre* I (1901) 180 ff.; a little differently Josef Kohler, *Lehrbuch der Rechtsphilosophie* (1909) 143. See also the authorities on administrative law mentioned by Thoma, "Rechtsstaatsidee" 199. Constantin Frantz, an opponent of liberalism, also pointed out the liberal content of the Just State in *Die Religion des Nationalliberalismus* (1872). The attitude of Jeremias Gotthelf, who attacked the liberal Rechtsstaat, was similar. See Schmitt, "Nationalsozialismus und Rechtsstaat" 714.

Although liberal ideology was prevalent in the nineteenth century, it became less popular as the century advanced. The concept of constitutionalism, as it was advanced by the "idealist of the Law State," Lasker, was soon competing with that of his fellow party member Bennigsen, "the idealist of the national state." [54] Jacoby's fight for the Just State was strongly opposed by Bismarck, who spoke derisively of the "artificial term Rechtsstaat which was invented by Robert von Mohl." [55] Von Stein and Gneist "by emphasizing a 'German' concept of constitutional government based upon the harmony of state and society, attempted with enormous exertions to prevent the subordination of the state to bourgeois society." [56] This means that they attempted to replace the liberal by a national ideology.[57] In the atmosphere of the unification of Germany, their attempts were successful. Nationalism increased at the cost of liberalism. The state again began to appear

[54] According to Thoma, *op. cit.* 200, these expressions were coined by Hermann Oncken.

[55] Bismarck spoke of "the artificial term Rechtsstaat which was invented by Robert von Mohl, a term of which there has not yet come into existence a definition that would satisfy a political mind, or a translation into foreign languages." To Gosler on Nov. 25, 1881. Quoted in Johannes Heckel, "Die Beilegung des Kulturkampfes in Preussen," *Zeitschrift der Savigny-Stiftung für Rechtsgeschichte* L (1930) 269.

[56] Schmitt, "Was bedeutet der Streit um den 'Rechtsstaat'?" 191. Comp. von Stein, *Die Verwaltungslehre* I, 1, 297, and Gneist, *Der Rechtsstaat* 180–82. Gneist, however, is not as free from liberal ideology as is indicated by Schmitt, "Was bedeutet der Streit um den 'Rechtsstaat'?" 191. For Gneist emphasizes "the *development of our economic life* to prosperity and a flourishing of civilization" as much as "*unity and greatness of the fatherland* in the united Germany." *Der Rechtsstaat* 1.

[57] Von Stein (*Verwaltungslehre* I, 1, 297 f.) and Gneist (*Der Rechtsstaat* 183 f., note 2) see in the word "Recht" in "Rechtsstaat" only positive law, not law in general or in the sense of justice.

32

more important than the law. The state's concept of justice was emphasized over the Just State.[58] In the end, the formula "Law State equals State Law" was accepted.[59] Constitutionalism no longer determined the content of State Law, but the latter determined the content of the former. The Law State became a mere positivistic statute state (*Gesetzesstaat*).[60] It thus could become a state that covered up unjust laws and injustice.

However, liberalism did not compete with national-

[58] On the primacy of the science of State Law due to the efforts of Gerber's *Grundzüge eines Systems des deutschen Staatsrechts* (1865) and Paul Laband's *Das Budgetrecht nach den Bestimmungen der preussischen Verfassungsurkunde* (1871) and *Das Staatsrecht des Deutschen Reiches* I (1876), see Hermann Rehm, *Geschichte der Staatsrechtswissenschaft* 261. Thoma, "Rechtsstaatsidee" 199, writes that the "ambiguous word" Rechtsstaat finally was discredited in the general *Staats-* and *Staatsrechtslehre* and refers to Bluntschli, von Seydel, Gareis, Rehm, and Bornhak.

[59] Schmitt, "Was bedeutet der Streit um den 'Rechtsstaat'?" 200, note 2, mentions the "abstract normativistic sophistry of Law State = State Law." Hans Kelsen, *Allgemeine Staatslehre* (1925) 44, 109, writes: "From a positivist point of view . . . the state is a king Midas for whom everything he touches becomes law. Therefore, from the point of view of legal positivism, every state must be a *Law* State in the sense that all state acts are acts of law, because and in so far as they realize an order which can be qualified as a *legal* order. . . . Whether power is determined by norms that have come about democratically or autocratically, the state always is an authority-state, there is always authority. And always the state is a Law State in the sense that a legal order determines that there shall be authority and how it shall be exercised, who is to give orders and who is to obey."

[60] Comp. Friedrich Darmstaedter, *Rechtsstaat oder Machtstaat* (1932) 85 ff.; Hayek, *Constitution of Liberty* 484, note 35; Schmitt, "Was bedeutet der Streit um den 'Rechtsstaat'?" 194, perhaps contradicting what he said in "Nationalsozialismus und Rechtsstaat" 715. Franz Neumann's statement that Rechtsstaat to the Germans merely implied the form through which each government could demonstrate its will overlooks the liberal content of the original Just State. On the other hand, Neumann admits that Mohl's concept of constitutionalism was not merely a formal one. "The Concept of Political Freedom," *Columbia Law Review* LIII (1953) 910 f.

ism only, but also with socialism. Whereas in the beginning national law was basically oriented toward individualism—the term "national-liberal" appears to be fitting because it expresses the prevalence of nationalism over liberalism, while it leaves little doubt about the liberal orientation of national law [61]—German law later became increasingly influenced by socialist ideas because of Bismarck's social legislation, the efforts of the "socialists of the chair" (professors with socialist inclinations), and the Social Democrats. In 1910, Thoma could well write: "Modern constitutionalism can be distinguished from that of the Middle Ages or of the Manchester school of economics, the nightwatchman state, which is supposed to be limited to the preservation of law and peace and not to interfere with the free play of the forces of society. This individualistic concept indeed no longer exists. The creative forces of national and social ideas have overcome it. This is often emphasized and nobody doubts it." [62]

Indeed nobody could well harbor doubts about it when the empire, which originally had been predominantly national-liberal, but had increasingly become social, was replaced by the Weimar Republic, which further enhanced nationalism and socialism. The increase of nationalism is not open to doubt. The Weimar constitution created a "decentralized unitary

[61] The expression "national-liberal" is not used here in the sense of the National Liberal Party. It should not be overlooked, however, that this party was formed in 1866 by men who, while not denying their liberal beliefs, supported the Prussian government in its national policy. Lasker was one of the founders of that party; Bennigsen later joined it.

[62] Thoma, "Rechtsstaatsidee" 199.

state" [63] whose federal remnants were soon attacked by a movement for centralization (*Reichsreform*).[64] As to the growth of the social element, the National Assembly of Weimar which drafted the constitution continued trends that had existed under the Empire. It incorporated into the constitution a bill of social rights, side by side with a bill of classic liberal rights.[65] As became evident in the course of the following years, liberal rights, among which those of property figured prominently, became subjected to severe regulations and infringements.[66] It is probably not much off the mark to maintain that by 1933 the Weimar Republic had become a national-social state [67] whose liberal elements had been considerably reduced. According to the prevalent opinion, all this came about in conformity with the principles of constitutionalism.[68] This shows to what degree liberal legitimacy had been replaced by a legal-

[63] Comp. Gerhard Anschütz, *Drei Leitgedanken der Weimarer Reichsverfassung* (1923) 12 ff.

[64] Comp. Walther Vogel, *Deutsche Reichsgliederung und Reichsreform in Vergangenheit und Gegenwart* (1932).

[65] Gerhard Anschütz, *Die Verfassung des Deutschen Reichs* (14th ed. 1933) 697 ff. Comp. also Ernst Rudolf Huber, "Bedeutungswandel der Grundrechte," *Archiv des öffentlichen Rechts* LXII (1933) 38 ff.; Carl Schmitt, *Verfassungslehre* (1928) 169 f.

[66] Comp. Anschütz, *Die Verfassung des Deutschen Reichs* 277 ff., 288 ff.

[67] The word is not used in the sense of the National Social Party, which was founded by Friedrich Naumann and others in 1896, although Naumann played a role in the drafting of the Weimar constitution which emphasized national and social elements.

[68] Comp. Anschütz, *Die Verfassung des Deutschen Reichs* 277 ff. Of a different opinion are Karl Loewenstein, "Zur Verfassungsmässigkeit der Notverordnungen vom Juli und August 1931," *Archiv des öffentlichen Rechts* LX (1932) 124 ff., and Fritz Morstein Marx, "Landesrechtliche Verwaltungsgerichtsbarkeit und Diktaturmassnahmen," *ibid.* LV (1929) 268 ff.

ity which, through an increasing abolition of liberal features, had degenerated into a mere statute-, regulation-, and emergency-regulation-state.[69]

The road from the national-social state to the national-socialist state was not long. Since the national-social Weimar Republic was considered constitutionalist, it is not surprising that the national-socialist Third Reich was. After all, it was basically a logical extension of its predecessor because its statism, denouncing what was liberal as "liberalistic," increased what was national into the "nationalistic," what was social into the "socialistic," and by virtue of *Gleichschaltung* or equalization further enhanced nationalistic and socialistic trends. Authors who still harbored some sympathy for liberalism and who realized that there could hardly be a Just State in the absence of some degree of liberalism, termed the Third Reich a Law State with emphasis upon the state.[70] One author considered subjecting national socialism to the tested methods of "relativization" and "emptying" (*Entleerung*) which are characteristic of the formal concept of constitutional government, and integrating it into the conceptual network of the normativistic Law State.[71] He asserted that in that case the "national-socialist state was without any doubt an exemplary Law State, perhaps even more so than there existed in any other country of the earth." [72] Opponents of liberalism saw in the Third Reich a

[69] Comp. the works mentioned in the preceding note, as well as Carl Schmitt, *Legalität und Legitimität* (1932).

[70] Schmitt, "Was bedeutet der Streit umd den 'Rechtsstaat'?" 196. Helfritz even tried to prove that the Third Reich was a Law State in the original meaning of that term. "Rechtsstaat und nationalsozialistischer Staat," *Deutsche Juristenzeitung* XXXIX (1934) 426 ff.

[71] Schmitt, "Was bedeutet der Streit um den 'Rechtsstaat'?" 197.

[72] Schmitt, "Nationalsozialismus und Rechtsstaat" 716.

"Weltanschauungsstaat which was oriented toward law and justice and no longer separated law and morals" [73] —the true Law State.[74] For them, the Hitler regime was a "national Law State," [75] a "national-socialist Law State," a "national-socialist German Rechtsstaat," [76] the "German Rechtsstaat of Adolf Hitler." [77]

IV

The Bonn Basic Law, providing for a "republican, democratic and social Law State," [78] did not succeed in establishing genuine constitutionalism.

We again consider the two competitors of liberalism —nationalism and socialism. There can be no doubt that

---

[73] Schmitt, "Was bedeutet der Streit um den 'Rechtsstaat'?" 198.

[74] Comp. Otto Koellreutter, *Der nationale Rechtsstaat* (1932), *Vom Sinn und Wesen der nationalen Revolution* (1933); Bodo Dennewitz, *Das nationale Deutschland ein Rechtsstaat* (1933); Hans Gerber, *Staatsrechtliche Grundlinien des Neuen Reiches* (1933); Heinrich Lange, *Vom Gesetzesstaat zum Rechtsstaat* (1934).

[75] Koellreutter, *op. cit.*; Dennewitz, *op. cit.*

[76] Lange, *op. cit.* 3; Schmitt, "Nationalsozialismus und Rechtsstaat" 716 f., "Was bedeutet der Streit um den 'Rechtsstaat'?" 199.

[77] Hans Frank, "Der deutsche Rechtsstaat Adolf Hitlers," *Deutsches Recht* IV (1934) 120; Schmitt, "Was bedeutet der Streit um den 'Rechtsstaat'?" 199. Lange, *op. cit.* 41, note 2, considers it "more than open to argument" that Forsthoff felt that the concept of the Law State was inapplicable to the Third Reich. Ernst Forsthoff stated later: "The history of the last forty years supplies remarkable and warning examples of the fact that concepts and institutions which were endangered in their existence were given all sorts of adjectives, such as the liberal, bourgeois, social, national and finally national-socialist Law State. They all connote stages of decline." "Begriff und Wesen des sozialen Rechtsstaates," *Veröffentlichungen der Vereinigung der Deutschen Staatsrechtslehrer* XII (1954) 15.

[78] Art. 28: "The constitutional order in the States must correspond to the principles of the republican, democratic and social Law State in the sense of this Basic Law."

the Basic Law is a reaction against nationalism. It rejects a centralized as well as a decentralized unitary state and provides for a federal state.[79] The situation is less clear with respect to the Basic Law's attitude toward socialism. Although the word "socialistic," which appeared in "national-socialistic," does not occur in the Basic Law, the word "social" does. The Basic Law not only refrains from opposing social trends as they existed in the Weimar Republic, but, as distinguished from the Weimar constitution, expressly refers to the state it creates as a social one. In view of this, its republican, democratic, and social Law State would be nothing but a new variation of the formal concept of constitutional government. Its substance would depend largely upon the interpretation of the word "social," since there is little doubt about the meaning of "republican" and "democratic." [80] If "social" is interpreted in the sense of social democracy, the Law State under the Basic Law would be a social-democratic one; if it is interpreted in the sense of Christian democracy, it would be a Christian-democratic one; if "social" is interpreted in the sense of liberalism, it would be a liberal one. Thus under the Basic Law constitutionalism can mean about anything, and about everything can be constitutionalist, as long as certain forms are being observed.[81]

Now the Federal Republic has been governed by Christian Democrats, Social Christians, and Liberals, and they all have interpreted the word "social" mainly

[79] Art. 20: "The Federal Republic of Germany is a democratic and social federal state." Comp. also the preamble and articles 1, 9, 25, 26.

[80] Forsthoff, *op. cit.* 23.

[81] An enumeration can be found in Scheuner, "Neuere Entwicklung des Rechtsstaats" 251 f.

in the sense of liberalism.[82] Should this practice continue, there could perhaps come about a modification of the constitution (*Verfassungswandlung*).[83] This could mean that sometime in the future the word "social" could no longer be interpreted in the sense of socialism.[84] Then a reaction against socialism would have been brought about which would be as far-reaching as that against nationalism. Those who applied the Basic Law would then have succeeded in doing what those who made that law did not dare, namely, to reconstruct a constitutional government similar to the one conceived by Mohl.[85] Although the Basic Law created a mere formal Law State, that state would have become a material one if it had consistently been filled up by liberal ideas. But this state of affairs probably has not yet been reached.

For the time being, the Federal Republic would then be constitutionalist not because the framers of the Basic Law believed in the original, substantive concept of the Law State, but because the government policy made it such a state. This means that the Federal Republic would be constitutionalist probably only as long

[82] Comp. Fritz Werner, "Sozialstaatliche Tendenzen in der Rechtsprechung," *Archiv des öffentlichen Rechts* LXXXI (1956) 84 ff.; Werner Thieme, "Liberalismus und Grundgesetz," *Zeitschrift für die gesamte Staatswissenschaft* CXIII (1957) 285 ff.

[83] Comp. Georg Jellinek, *Verfassungsänderung und Verfassungswandlung* (1906).

[84] Perhaps the Godesberg Program of the Social Democratic Party supports this opinion.

[85] And perhaps also comes close to the ideal of Stahl if one takes into consideration the Christian aspects of the Basic Law, which were, however, seldom emphasized since the adoption of that law. Comp. my "Natural Law in the Modern European Constitutions," *Natural Law Forum* I (1956) 73 ff.

as Christian Democrats, Social Christians, and Liberals constitute the government. Should the government change, the Federal Republic could become a Law State in the sense of the new or old Social Democracy. The life-expectancy of the present "social" Law-State, which comes close to the originally conceived concept of constitutional government, would thus be only a matter of time, which, however, in no way jeopardizes the existence of the Basic Law.

Or does the Basic Law itself bid farewell to the merely formal concept of constitutionalism? [86] Does it expressly provide for a liberal Just State,[87] so that it would stand or fall with the existence of such a state? Did governmental practice merely follow the Basic Law? Wasn't it necessary to fill a formal Law State with a liberal substance because the Basic Law itself provided for such a substance? There are indications of this fact. As distinguished from the constitutions of the Empire and the Weimar Republic, the Basic Law mentions the word "Law State." This indicates a desire to preclude a formalization and falsification as was possible under the other constitutions, perhaps because they omitted the word "Law State." [88] Provisions of the Basic Law, securing freedom in a larger measure than previous constitutions, support this opinion. We have in

[86] This question is answered in the affirmative by Christian Friedrich Menger, *Der Begriff des sozialen Rechtsstaats im Bonner Grundgesetz* (1953) 17, and by Scheuner, "Neuere Entwicklung" 230 ff., 247 ff., who considers this opinion the ruling one.

[87] Tending toward this opinion Friedrich Klein, "Bonner Grundgesetz und Rechtsstaat," *Zeitschrift für die gesamte Staatswissenschaft* CVI (1950) 390 ff.; Menger, *op. cit.* (comp. the remarks by Erich Fechner, *Freiheit und Zwang im sozialen Rechtsstaat* [1953] 8); Thieme, "Liberalismus und Grundgesetz."

[88] Comp. Klein, *op. cit.* 390; Scheuner, *op. cit.* 230.

mind the protection of basic rights, federalism and democracy as they are evident, especially in articles 1, 3, 9, 18, 19, 20, and 79. Since not only the executive and judicial, but also the legislative and even the amending, powers are restricted by liberal principles, much seems to have been done indeed to secure the primacy of law and justice over the state, freedom over power, and constitutionalism over the positive law of the state.

The word "social" before "Law State" in the text of the Basic Law could then simply be understood in the sense of the classic social contract. It would then be quite compatible with liberalism, signifying that the Bonn Law State is a state which in a truly social manner gives to everyone the opportunity to make use of his abilities and to earn the results of his efforts. It could be emphasized that as an adjective "social" is subordinated to the substantive "Law State," that "social Law State" cannot possibly imply an equality between the social state and the Law State.[89] Since the

[89] A social state, as existing under the Basic Law, is mentioned by Fechner, *op. cit.;* Hans Gerber, "Die Sozialstaatsklausel des Grundgesetzes," *Archiv des öffentlichen Rechts* LXXXI (1956) 1 ff.; Hans Peter Ipsen, "Enteignung und Sozialisierung," *Veröffentlichungen der Vereinigung der Deutschen Staatsrechtslehrer* X (1952) 74 ff.; Wilhelm Reuss, Kurt Jantz, *Sozialstaatsprinzip und soziale Sicherheit* (1960); Scheuner, *op. cit.* In 1931, Heinrich Triepel stated: "Many legal ideas which were emphasized and developed by liberalism, even the most valuable ones, are not specifically liberal. They are much older than liberalism, have survived liberalism and will survive us. If the timeless Law State is given the attribute 'liberal', something that is usually done in order to denounce the Law State; if with the same purpose in mind one speaks of the 'bourgeois' Law State to signify the Law State of the bourgeoisie which fears for its 'security'; if, in distinction to that kind of Law State, one construes a 'social' Law State; it can only be said that all these are distortions against which we, men of the law, all of whom it is hoped favor the Law State, ought to protest. For here an eternal value is pulled down into the dust of finite-littleness." *Veröffentlichungen der Vereinigung der*

substantive "federal state" also appears in connection with the adjective "social" (Art. 20), it could further be argued that the substantives "federal state" and "Law State" constitute higher values in the Basic Law than the adjectives "democratic" and "social," that the pairing of "federal state and Law State"—complementary and harmonious from the point of view of freedom [90]— is superior to the pairing of "democratic and social"— complementary and harmonious from the point of view of social dependence.[91]

However, this interpretation, derived from a harmony of provisions of the Basic Law, which concern essential features of the Federal Republic, is not the ruling one. Although it would have been possible to make it such by arguing that the law is wiser than its creator,[92] people failed to do so. To bring about such an interpretation would probably have necessitated a *tour de force*, similar to the one employed by Chief Justice Marshall when he established judicial review and thus secured the primacy of the rule of law before that of men in the United States for a long time to

---

Deutschen Staatsrechtslehrer VII (1932) 197. Comp. also Menger, *op. cit.* 6; Forsthoff, "Begriff und Wesen des sozialen Rechtsstaates" 15.

[90] The classic work on this pairing is probably *The Federalist*. In modern times, Swiss authors have excelled in pointing out the value of federalism for constitutionalism. Comp. Georg Messmer, *Föderalismus und Demokratie* (1946); Hans Haug, "Föderalismus und Demokratie," *Neue Schweizer Rundschau* XII (N.F. 1954) 131 ff.; Martin Usteri, *Theorie des Bundesstaates* (1954). Wilhelm Röpke also shares this opinion, see his *Jenseits von Angebot und Nachfrage* (1958). Comp. also my "Economic Rights and Federalism in the United States," *South African Law Journal* LXXXIII (1966) 60 ff.

[91] Here also the classic work is *The Federalist*. The naturalness of this pairing was also emphasized in my *In Defense of Property* 128 ff.

[92] Gustav Radbruch, *Rechtsphilosophie* (6th ed. 1963) 210 f.

come.[93] Had such a *tour de force* taken place in Germany, it could perhaps have prevented the possibility that one day social elements will deal the *coup de grace* to the constitutionalist elements of the Basic Law. However, great decisions against the democratic tide are rare in a democracy.

It would be unfair to reproach anyone for the fact that no ruling interpretation of the Basic Law came about which made explicit the primacy of the individualistic liberal Just State and thus restored that state.[94] For the social aspects of the Basic Law are quite strong. When the Basic Law was drafted and ratified, the word "social" was predominantly interpreted in the sense of socialism. It was opposed to "liberal." Without any doubt, this was the opinion of the Marxists. Their opinion was shared by quite a few members of the bourgeois parties. The majority of the members of the Parliamentary Council probably did not consider an

[93] Marbury v. Madison, 5 U.S. (1 Cranch) 137 (1803). Marshall here follows Hamilton's essay 78 in *The Federalist*. Comp. Oliver Wendell Holmes, *Collected Legal Papers* (1920) 269: "I should feel a . . . doubt whether, after Hamilton and the Constitution itself, Marshall's work proved more than a strong intellect, a good style, personal ascendancy in his court, courage, justice and the convictions of his party." Thomas Jefferson saw in the Supreme Court a "citadel of public justice" from which "all the works" of egalitarian democracy would be "beaten down and erased." To John Dickinson on Dec. 19, 1801, *The Writings of Thomas Jefferson* X (Mem. ed. 1903) 302. The decline of judicial review in the United States since 1937 is discussed in my "America and Europe—Decline and Emergence of Judicial Review," *Virginia Law Review* XLIV (1958) 1233 ff.; also *South African Law Journal* LXXVI (1959) 398 ff.

[94] This restoration is assumed by Fechner, *Freiheit und Zwang* 10; Helmut Rumpf, *Der ideologische Gehalt des Bonner Grundgesetzes* (1958) 28; Thieme, "Liberalismus und Grundgesetz" 291. It is denied by Otto Bachof, "Begriff und Wesen des sozialen Rechtsstaates," *Veröffentlichungen der Vereinigung der Deutschen Staatsrechtslehrer* XII (1954) 38.

43

absolute abolition of laws providing for socialism and planning, as they had been adopted during the Empire, the Weimar Republic, and even the Third Reich. In contrast to earlier German constitutions, the Basic Law expressly refers to the republic it establishes as a "social federal state" and a "social Law State." It is true that the liberal bill of rights is not matched in the Basic Law by a bill of social rights. However, this omission is amply compensated by general social clauses (*Sozialklauseln*) because a "flight" into these clauses [95] appears to be possible. Thus the very fact that "the Basic Law expresses socialism (*Sozialstaatlichkeit*) only as an urgent program, without specifying its principles and ways of realization," [96] and thus does not limit it, could more easily lead to the establishment of socialism than a specific bill of social rights. [97] Therefore, if the Basic Law provides for a substantive constitutionalism at all, it provides at best for a hybrid, a *Zwitterding*, a predominantly liberal-social state. [98]

[95] Justus Wilhelm Hedemann, *Die Flucht in die Generalklauseln* (1933), subtitles his study "A Danger to Law and State." In the years following the publication of this book it was demonstrated how a flight into the general clauses of private law was followed by one into the general clauses of public law. The results of the national-socialist general clause of "the sound sentiment of the people" (*gesundes Volksempfinden*) were too terrible to permit us not to fear the potential results of a social general clause.

[96] Gustav Radbruch, *Einführung in die Rechtswissenschaft* (9th ed. by Konrad Zweigert 1958) 83 f. In the same sentence can be read that the idea of the social state "pushes victoriously toward its realization."

[97] Comp. Walter Hamel, *Die Bedeutung der Grundrechte im sozialen Rechtsstaat* (1957). Already in essay 84 of *The Federalist*, Hamilton stressed that a bill of rights could be to the disadvantage of the individual on account of its enumeration of certain rights, which amounts to a limitation of the individual's freedom to these rights.

[98] Comp. Fechner, *Freiheit und Zwang* 5: "The term 'social' is . . . in the connection 'social Just State' as new as it is dubious." Rumpf,

However, such a hybrid is problematic on account of the basic antinomy between liberal and social ideas,[99] ideas which oppose and neutralize each other and thus can de-materialize constitutional government. The conclusion can thus be drawn that the Basic Law provides for a formal type of constitutionalism only and leaves it up to the government to substantiate that type with its respective program, i.e., to determine it by means of State Law. Within the framework of the Basic Law, this makes possible a liberal or social, Christian-democratic, Christian-social, liberal-democratic, or social-democratic Law State, or one based upon combinations of these ideas or parties in small and great coalitions, one which is influenced by their values, values which can neutralize each other and thus nullify the Law State.

V

The preceding survey shows that the Just State has not regained its primacy over the state's own concept of justice. Constitutional government is as much deter-

---

op. cit. 27, writes: "The idea of the Just State and that of the social state are connected in the Basic Law to the vague constitutional concept of the social Rechtsstaat, the meaning of which is dubious." The dubiousness of the concept "social Just State" probably is what is the least doubtful about it. Surveys on the various interpretations, which reach from emphasis upon liberalism to emphasis upon socialism, can be found in Gerber, "Die Sozialstaatsklausel des Grundgesetzes," and Reuss/Jantz, *op. cit.* 7 ff.

[99] This antinomy is emphasized by Forsthoff, "Begriff und Wesen des sozialen Rechtsstaates," and Klein, "Bonner Grundgesetz und Rechtsstaat." Bachof, "Begriff und Wesen des sozialen Rechtsstaates" 80, speaks of a limited antinomy. Rumpf, *op. cit.* 28, writes that whereas one could think of a theoretical connection between the Just State and the social state, this could not be done in practice because the two are incompatible.

mined today by the law of the Federal Republic as it was previously by the law of the Weimar Republic and the Empire, i.e., by temporary beliefs. The great variety of these beliefs shows that in spite of an acceptance of the merely formal concept of the Law State the classic ideal of that state can be approached pretty closely. On the other hand, it shows how far one can move away from that ideal and how much it is possible to conceal under the cover of constitutionalism a despotic state whose law makes a farce out of justice and establishes a state of injustice. It shows how behind the rule of law there can be concealed the best and worst rule of men.

This leaves the question concerning the future of constitutionalism. It is an uneasy question. The answer offers, I think, little encouragement. In 1929, Walter Jellinek wrote: "During the war and the first years thereafter a powerful wave of the police state went through the land. . . . Already voices could be heard claiming that the days of the Law State were numbered, that as a liberal institution it was a thing of the past and that it must make room for a new strengthening of state power. Also, the examples of Russia, which after overcoming the Czarist police state introduced the even more ruthless Soviet police state, and fascism, had to give us pause. In spite of everything Germany will remain constitutionalist. A people that brought forth the story of Michael Kohlhaas, created the *Rütli* scene, handed down the answer of the miller of Sanssouci from generation to generation, wrung judicial independence from the government through martyrdom, will not let themselves be deprived of their ideal by foreign influences or temporary exigencies. Knowledgeable men also have recognized for some time that an orderly legal protection strengthens the cause of the state and thus the power of the government. The epoch of constitutionalism will thus prevail for the foreseeable future." [100]

These words were written from the vantage point of a republic which was considered an example of democracy by a scholar who saw in democracy a guaranty for liberal rights, shortly before a new wave of the police state went through Germany, a wave which became despotic after 1933. And whereas Jellinek's words demonstrate a firm belief in the genuine Just State, they also indicate an acceptance of the merely formal concept of constitutionalism, a concept he approves of as long as its substance is determined democratically. Jellinek's confidence in democracy obviously was so great that he did not mind a strengthening of the idea of the state and its power, as long as both rested on a democratic basis.[101] Thus wrote a professor of State Law for whom democratic law could hardly jeopardize constitutional government.

On the other hand, in view of the experiences in Germany after 1929 and in other democracies earlier, we are prompted to fear a strengthening of governmental power in democracies no less than under other forms of government. Democracy can be the best as well as the worst form of government. If it is the former, it is probably also the most difficult. It is to Gerhard Leibholz's credit that he drew attention to the dangers of "democ-

[100] Walter Jellinek, *Verwaltungsrecht* (2d ed. 1929) 91.
[101] The just-quoted passage appears unchanged in the third edition of 1931, 96 f.

ratism," which emphasizes social rights at the cost of liberal ones.[102] Democratism threatens constitutionalism, for democracy, like other forms of government, contains the germ of degeneration into a state of might, arbitrariness, and injustice. Leibholz probably wrote as a professor of political science rather than a professor of State Law.

It is perhaps significant that the development of a liberal constitutionalism under the Basic Law occurred at a time when political science was reinstituted in Germany. That science had been flourishing in Mohl's time, but later was discredited with the emergence of the science of State Law. Whereas politics seeks power at the cost of justice, political science emphasizes the restriction of power for the sake of justice. Thus political science is sympathetic to the Law State, the rule of law as distinguished from that of men. It is its natural ally. It is perhaps no mere coincidence that many of its present representatives in Germany returned from classic nations of the rule of law to their mother country, which they left at a time when politics was so predomi-

---

[102] The "tension between liberal and so-called social basic rights can in the final analysis not be solved because it makes evident the tension between liberalism and democratism. The more a system of social basic rights is perfected, the narrower becomes the room in which liberal basic rights can exist." *Strukturprinzipien des modernen Verfassungsstaates* (1965) 15. Forty years earlier, Leibholz had pointed out the antinomy of liberalism and democratism in *Die Gleichheit vor dem Gesetz* (1925) 17. A few years thereafter, he pointed out the antinomy of "liberalistic" and "social" by emphasizing the basic affinity between liberalism and the Just State. "Die Wahlrechtsreform und ihre Grundlagen," *Veröffentlichungen der Vereinigung der Deutschen Staatsrechtslehrer* VII (1932) 165. Comp. also *Die Gleichheit vor dem Gesetz* 70 f., where Leibholz admits a right of resistance even in the Law State, against the prevalent opinion of the representatives of State Law.

nant that the science of State Law could flourish, but not political science.[103]

Whether political science will be able to save constitutional government, is, however, another question. It seems as if it is becoming a mere yesman to politics, just as earlier the science of State Law did not so much ask whether what is also ought to be, but was content with describing and, at best, interpreting existing law. Political science has increasingly become value-free and quantitative.[104] As such, it is well suited to the merely formal concept of constitutionalism. Hence political science, having become value-free, will probably be as unable as politics to withstand the democratic tide. It will follow in the footsteps of the science of State Law and succumb to that law. Political science will then accept every substance with which democratic governments will fill the formal Law State according to the principle *tel est notre plaisir*.[105] Since the democratic ruler is insatiable, that ruler will assume more and more power. In the end, the formal Law State will be mere window-dressing for a democratic power- and police-state, characterized by such a mass of statutes, rules, and regulations that not much will be left of the libertarian substance of genuine constitutionalism.

Bismarck called "Law State" an "artificial term." This is not surprising from a power-politician. The politician will consider many things artificial which the political

[103] We think of Arnold Bergstraesser, Heinrich Brüning, Ernst Fraenkel, Carl Joachim Friedrich, Gerhard Leibholz, and Eric Voegelin.

[104] Opposed to this trend are Eric Voegelin, *The New Science of Politics* (1952), and Carl J. Friedrich, *Man and his Government* (1963).

[105] Comp. Gerhard Anschütz, "Deutsches Staatsrecht" in Holtzendorff/Kohler, *Encyklopädie der Rechtswissenschaft* II (1904) 593.

scientist will value as artistic. The Law State is more artistic than State Law, in so far as it is more difficult to make the state bow to the law than the other way around. Justice is so delicate a thing that it can easily be hurt, even through laws. In order to thrive, the Just State needs an artistic structure of the state, a structure that existed during the period of constitutionalism when governmental power was divided and restricted to the preservation of peace and freedom. The structure of constitutional government is tender. Exercise of power threatens to crush it. Therefore, it probably is safest under the kind of *laissez-faire* which existed at the time that type of government was conceived in Germany. The Law State thus appears to be a historical concept, which perhaps cannot be adjusted to new political ideas and programs.[106] It requires a certain atmosphere. Such an atmosphere hardly exists in the twentieth century, which is characterized by an accumulation of governmental power and a mass of state interventions.

Still, it would be wrong simply to discard constitutionalism as a thing of the past. The present always has sought comfort in the past. "Idealists of the Law State," often denounced and discredited, in an admirable way have tried again and again to defend freedom against state power as it was reflected in State Law, by emphasizing the principles of constitutional government. Their efforts were by no means without results. Perhaps there is consolation in the thought that the ideal of the liberal Just State was probably never absolutely reached even in the nineteenth century, and that, on the other hand, it was at times approached quite closely in the twentieth century. There will probably always be trends to-

[106] Comp. Julius Binder, *Der deutsche Volksstaat* (1934) 17.

ward constitutionalism as a reaction against trends toward the police state. Just as there is a fluctuation between natural and positive law,[107] such a movement probably also exists between the major variations of the rule of law—the Law State and State Law. Therefore, idealists of the former will merit our admiration also in the future, the more so since in all probability they will fight for a lost cause in the social, democratic tide.

For in the last analysis, fewer limitations are set on democracy than on other forms of government. Thus democratic law can do to the Law State whatever pleases the people.[108] How it will do this in particular, remains to be seen. *Omen cum nomen?*

[107] Comp. Heinrich Rommen, *Die ewige Wiederkehr des Naturrechts* (2d ed. 1947).
[108] Comp. Leibholz, *Die Gleichheit vor dem Gesetz* 146.

II

STATE JUSTICE
AND
THE JUST STATE

FROM THE POINT OF VIEW of content, State Law often appeared as an inversion of the Law State. Functionally, however, the situation is different: The former has the task of creating and of securing the latter with the help of the police. Without State Law, there can be no Law State.

I

Our love for the Just State must not degenerate into sentimentalizing that state out of existence, for such a perversion can easily lead to the twilight of constitutional government. Measure and mean.[1]

The danger of such sentimentalizing is especially great in a democracy. Especially under that form of government, the friends of constitutionalism must be-

[1] See Wilhelm Röpke, *Mass und Mitte* (1950). As to permissiveness, dealt with in the following pages, comp. his *Torheiten der Zeit* (1966) 9 ff.

ware of permitting their idealism to become unduly permissive. They must guard not only against the democratic tide, which can result in the oppression of the individual by the power of the state, but also against democratic trends toward the dissolution of the legal and political order. Democracy is a difficult form of government: aside from its good constitutionalist aspect, there are two bad aspects which threaten to crush and make unrecognizable the golden mean of constitutionalism. First, the despotism of the compact majority; second, the improper permissiveness that drifts toward anarchy under the pluralistic "government" of an atomized society in which everybody can behave and misbehave according to the principle, *tel est mon plaisir.* Just as the despotic variant of democracy all too often has jeopardized human rights, its permissive variant threatens these rights by exposing citizens to the crimes of their fellow-men. Democracy can become the sorcerer's apprentice of liberalism not only through unlimited majority rule, but also through licentiousness.

These dangers must be emphasized especially in the case of social democracy, considered by many the only genuine form of democracy. Social democracy can, of course, be despotic, owing to its regulatory planning as well as the consolidation of the structure of the state and the enlargement of state power that go with it. However, due to its deterministic philosophy, social democracy also will find it hard not to wink at the illegal behavior of its citizens, especially with respect to private property. It will thus aid lawlessness.[2] The history of socialism is a history of anarchism as well as of des-

[2] Comp. Friedrich A. Hayek, *The Road to Serfdom* (1944); the author's *In Defense of Property* 99 ff., 153 ff.

potism. In other words, social democracy is a potential threat to constitutionalism not only because it rejects *laissez-faire*, in the sense of Adam Smith, but also because it attempts to explain misdemeanors and crimes by faults in the social structure. It thus creates a kind of *laissez-passer* in which everything goes, and even manslaughter and murder are generously forgiven. A behavior which Welzel would consider inadmissible from the point of view of social ethics [3] is transformed into a behavior which supposedly is caused by an environment that is unbearable from the point of view of social ethics. This environment is said to be unbearable mainly because it still contains genuine liberal features. The night-watchman state, which merely provided for a minimum of interference into the private lives of its citizens and yet was courageous enough to strictly enforce its laws and to preserve justice for the people, will be rejected by those who with Marx believe that laws merely protect the economically strong from the economically weak and legalize "social injustice." Law and order are thus undermined. The protection of the underdog, advocated by an appeal to "social justice" and the "social conscience," leads to a dog's life for law-abiding and peace-loving citizens who must live in permanent fear of rowdies who, as an American candidate for the presidency said, are out of custody before their victims can even think of leaving the hospital.[4]

In spite of all the dangers to which law is exposed in

[3] Hans Welzel, *Das Deutsche Strafrecht* (11th ed. 1969) 1 ff.

[4] However one may feel toward George C. Wallace, it is his merit of having clearly stated the decline of law and order and the dangers to the existence of the United States resulting from it. Thereupon, the law-and-order issue was also taken up by Richard Nixon and perhaps helped him to win the election.

the authoritarian state, it should never be forgotten that John Locke's remarks about law in the state of nature are utopian.[5] As Abraham Lincoln stated at the beginning of his political career, there is no justice in an anarchy. A community in which the laws are not enforced must perish.[6] Even authors known for their resistance to state intervention have left no doubt about the necessity of obeying the laws.[7] Clearly, an abundance of legislation is risky because it creates legal chaos and insecurity and results in undue restrictions of freedom. However, the non-enforcement of existing laws by the executive power also is dangerous.[8] Negation of the laws endangers the Just State as much as does a mania for legislation. As far as the execution of the laws is concerned, a rule of law is hardly conceivable without the rule of men.

Interested as it mainly is in the freedom of the individual from the power of the state, political science can probably do less in this situation than State Law, which mainly aims at the maintenance of state authority. Of course, it is possible that law provides for a permissiveness which goes beyond an orderly protection of human

[5] John Locke, *Two Treatises of Government* (2d Laslett ed. 1967) 69, 97 ff., 287 ff.

[6] Address Before the Young Men's Lyceum of Springfield, Ill., January 27, 1838. *The Collected Works of Abraham Lincoln* (Basler ed. 1953) I, 108 ff.

[7] Comp. Wilhelm Röpke's letter of August 18, 1952, to Pierre F. Goodrich: "Lord Acton certainly did not mean to deny that, if there is something worse than despotism, it is anarchy, i.e. the absence of power."

[8] This is clearly expressed by Hamilton and Madison in *The Federalist*, esp. in essays 62 and 70, also in essays 13, 21, 26, 37, 49, 51. Comp. also the author's *The Federalist* 109, 115, 120 f., 131, 150 f., 163, 228 f., 248.

rights and leads to anarchy. However, this is unlikely to happen frequently. Constitution-makers seldom will create law which is not viable, just as a sound political science will not protect the individual to a degree that endangers the community, if only because the destruction of the *polis* would end political science. Conscientious suicide generally can be found as little among scientists as among politicians. On the other hand, it must not be overlooked that, seen from the viability of the existing, law is less in jeopardy than science, which always is interested in innovation.[9] Whatever it may look like and however it may collide with the ideal Just State, the law of any given state always will stand for certain values, among which there will be that of order even if the proposed order is an extremely fragile one. In contrast, political science in the sense of scientism can be value-free. As a matter of fact, it has become increasingly value-free. As a result, its representatives not only have been satisfied with the mere description and enumeration of facts, but also have favored a *laissez-passer* under which everybody can use his own standard of values even if this leads to lawlessness.

It is a merit of Carl Joachim Friedrich to have drawn attention to the danger of anarchism which through permissiveness jeopardizes constitutional government. Democracy threatens constitutionalism: tending toward permissiveness, it contains the seeds of the realization of man's lust for power, arbitrariness, and injustice. Friedrich thus is a political scientist who has resisted

[9] Comp. the author's *Youth, University and Democracy* (1970) 57 ff.

dangerous trends within his profession and who has also been, as much as seems to be necessary, a believer in State Law.[10]

[10] As to the problem of "value-free," compare esp. his *Man and His Government* (1963). At the beginning of his publications there can be found, next to works on constitutionalist institutions, such as "The Issue of Judicial Review in Germany," *Political Science Quarterly* XLIII (1928) 188 ff., and *Politica Methodica Digesta of Johannes Althusius* (1932), studies which emphasize the sanction of constitutionalist institutions by State Law. His contribution, "The German and the Prussian Civil Service," in L. D. White, ed., *The Civil Service in the Modern State* (1930), is followed by a defense of Art. 48 of the Weimar constitution: "The very nature of this form of government, based as it is upon a separation of powers and legislation after extensive discussion and negotiation with all interested groups, is peculiarly in need of extraordinary arrangements whenever an imminent danger requires immediate action. The real reason for such arrangements as are made by Article 48 is the preservation of the constitutional fabric as a whole by temporarily dispensing with certain parts of it." While the "crisis through which Germany has been passing does not at all imply the establishment of a dictatorship," Friedrich emphasizes, in view of national-socialist and communist threats to public security and order: "Truly benevolent despotism of this sort forestalls internal chaos and a complete breakdown of the government, particularly when it is placed in the hands of a man who has grown old in unswerving loyalty and service to his country." "Dictatorship in Germany?", *Foreign Affairs* IX (1930) 128, 131, 132. "The Development of the Executive Power in Germany," *American Political Science Review* XXVII (1933), stresses that "even in time of peace a national emergency will call forth executive leadership in more or less dictatorial forms. . . . dictatorship is the natural concomitant of democracy in times of stress and strain." He ends by saying: "In any case, Germany will remain a constitutional, democratic state with strong socializing tendencies whose backbone will continue to be its professional civil service" (190, 203). Although this hope was not fulfilled, Friedrich did not waver in his opinion that constitutional government presupposes the sanction by State Law. His *Constitutional Government and Democracy* (originally published under the title *Constitutional Government and Politics*), which deals with the freedom of the individual in the Law State, in all editions (1937, 1941, 1946, 1950, 1968) not only takes for granted a general obedience to the laws, but also justifies emergency measures.

Friedrich thus is a student of Robert von Mohl, a teacher of State Law considered by many the father of the concept of the Just State. Friedrich expressly acknowledged Mohl's methods in his *Der Verfas-*

He had good reason to be that way. When, in the last years of the Weimar Republic, Walter Jellinek denied that constitutional government, a liberal institution, had seen its day and had to make room for a new strengthening of state power, the National Socialists who, like the Communists, wanted to overthrow the republic, had already spread. The end of the republic through Hitler's accession to power probably was due to no small degree to the fact that the Weimar Republic, democratic as it was and ruled as it was by Social Democrats, not only harbored trends toward despotism, but also toward anarchy. There was a lax execution of criminal law, probably influenced by Radbruch's proposals for a reform of criminal law. An increased criminality and a growing disorder, resulting from riots, followed. These, in turn, led to a growth of "order-parties" such as the National

---

sungsstaat der Neuzeit (1953) vii. The latter work has for its theme Hölderlin's words:
Wie auf schlanken Säulen ruh'
auf richt'gen Ordnungen das neue Leben,
Und euern Bund befest'ge das Gesetz.
As on slender columns should rest
on right orders the new life,
and your alliance be cemented by the law.
Friedrich also acted in the spirit of a great American scholar and friend of constitutionalism, Charles H. McIlwain, who could have celebrated his 100th birthday this year and preceded Carl Joachim Friedrich as Eaton Professor of the Science of Government. McIlwain's work (The Political Works of James I [1918]; The American Revolution: A Constitutional Interpretation [1923]; Christopher Goodman, How superior powers oght to be obeyd of their subiects wherin they may lawfully by Gods worde be disobeyed and resisted [1931]; The Growth of Political Thought in the West from the Greeks to the End of the Middle Ages [1932]; The High Court of Parliament and Its Supremacy [1934]; Constitutionalism, Ancient and Modern [1940]) also shows that he was a believer in both the Law State and State Law, a combination characteristic of Friedrich, a political scientist who at the same time was a member of a department of government and of a faculty of law.

Socialists and the Communists.[11] When Jellinek on the one hand has reservations about "a new strengthening of state power" and, on the other hand, emphasizes "that an orderly protection of the law strengthens the idea of the state and, thereby, the power of the state" (thus depicting state power, as it is established by State Law, as a *conditio sine qua non* of constitutional government),[12] he shows the dilemma of a liberal democrat who is afraid of state power and yet considers such power necessary because it not only restricts, but also protects, the citizen.

The experience of the Weimar Republic has shown that sentimentalizing constitutionalism out of existence is as bad as fighting it openly. As Schmitt emphasized with most scholars, the formal Law State of the Weimar constitution was predominantly liberal[13] and thus came close to the ideal Law State. On the other hand, it contained national and social features which were detrimental to that ideal.[14] It often has been stressed that on account of institutions such as the right of the lawmaker to restrict basic rights, and the power of the Reich President, the Weimar Republic was in constant danger of degenerating into despotism, be it that of the majority, of the Reich President, or of the latter acting for the majority. It should not be overlooked, however, that the tragedy of the Weimar Republic was also caused by its inclination toward permissiveness.

[11] Comp. Heinrich Brüning, *Memoiren 1918–1934* (1970).
[12] Jellinek, *Verwaltungsrecht* (3rd ed. 1931) 96 f.
[13] Carl Schmitt, *Verfassungslehre* (1928) 30 f.
[14] See *supra*, 34 ff.

II

Under the "democratic and social Law State" of the Bonn Basic Law (Art. 28), the Federal Republic of Germany has not been sufficiently protected from anarchism.

Viewing the constitutions made after World War II, the Basic Law deserves praise. In contrast to the constitution of the Fourth Republic, which is very similar to that of the Third Republic, and to the constitution of the Italian Republic, which is very similar to the *Statuto*, the Basic Law shows important improvements over its democratic predecessor, the constitution of the Weimar Republic.[15] Obviously, the Parliamentary Council which drafted the Basic Law, had learned from the mistakes made by the National Assembly that drafted the Weimar constitution, as well as by the experiences under that constitution. Nevertheless, the Basic Law contains provisions which from the point of view of constitutionalism are not without risk. Since the possibilities of despotism under the Basic Law have already been pointed out,[16] we shall now restrict ourselves to dealing with those of anarchy. If one now thinks of the parallels between constitutional development in Germany and the United States—we have in mind not only good American influences upon the Basic Law and the less laudable impact of demonstrations and riots, all of which seem to verify Max Weber's prediction that

[15] Comp. the author's "Natural Law in the Modern European Constitutions" 73 ff.; "The Federal Republic of Germany: An Evaluation After Ten Years," *Journal of Politics* XXII (1960) 112 ff.

[16] See *supra*, 25 ff.

our life will become Americanized [17]—one must grow exceedingly uneasy, especially if one takes into account Hans Huber's thesis that constitutional development progresses faster in Germany than in the United States.[18]

Advanced in connection with the decline of liberalism, that thesis corresponded only too much to the facts. When it was voiced, the federal state of the Empire, conducive as it was to freedom, already had been replaced by Hitler's centralization, while the United States still was a federal state whose citizens enjoyed substantial liberties. However, as a result of the New Deal and the New Frontier, there spread, under the Warren Court,[19] a permissiveness which made the decade President Kennedy envisaged as the golden sixties the most terrible period since the Civil War, costing him, his brother, Martin Luther King, and many peace-loving citizens their lives at the hands of murderers. In view of this, the thought that in Germany permissiveness would show its results even faster and in a more terrible way must make the question as to where the Federal Republic is drifting even more agonizing now than at the time it was asked by Jaspers.[20]

The Parliamentary Council can hardly be blamed for

[17] Max Weber, *Wissenschaft als Beruf* (1919) in *Gesammelte Aufsätze zur Wissenschaftslehre* (2d ed. 1951) 568. The American influence can clearly be seen with a constitutionalist like Robert von Mohl. It is also evident in the German literature on State Law during the 19th century, especially with respect to federalism.

[18] Hans Huber, "Ueber Foederalismus," *Neue Schweizer Rundschau* VI (1938) 241 ff.

[19] Comp. Alpheus T. Mason, "Understanding the Warren Court: Judicial Self-restraint and Judicial Duty," *Political Science Quarterly* LXXXI (1966) 523 ff.

[20] Karl Jaspers, *Wohin treibt die Bundesrepublik?* (1966), fears despotism, but not anarchy.

this situation. It sincerely tried to build a stable republic. Following the United States constitution as well as the constitutions of the Fourth Republic and of the Republic of Italy,[21] the Basic Law, in order to safeguard the public order, even restricts the amending power (Art. 79). In spite of a far-reaching protection of basic rights, these rights cannot be claimed by those who abuse them in order to attack the free, democratic basic order.[22] Associations which are directed against the constitutional order shall be prohibited (Art. 9). Parties which, according to their aims and the behavior of their members, seek to impair or abolish the free and democratic order or to jeopardize the existence of the Federal Republic can be declared unconstitutional (Art. 21).

This far-reaching protection of the Federal Republic and its constitutionalist features is complemented by a consolidation of parliamentary government. While the constitutions of the Fourth Republic and the Italian Republic hardly improve the instability characteristic of their democratic predecessors,[23] the Basic Law, by providing for the constructive vote of non-confidence (Art. 67), enriches parliamentary government by an important stabilizing institution. Experience has shown that the Federal Chancellor has a mandate similar to that of the American President. The Federal Republic became known as a "chancellor's democracy." Erhard's fall is

[21] U. S. constitution, art. 5; constitution of the Fourth Republic, art. 95; constitution of the Italian Republic, art. 139.

[22] See also art. 17a.

[23] Art. 51 of the French constitution of 1946 provides for a dissolution of the National Assemby if there are two government crises within 18 months. It was used only once and hardly stabilized French governments whose duration during the Third Republic was, on the average, about 9 months.

the exception which confirms the rule. Even that event was not a traditional parliamentary crisis with its typical feature, the absence of government.

In spite of these provisions, however, it appears dubious whether under the Basic Law anarchism will be handled successfully. Stabilizing as the constructive vote of non-confidence may be, the Chancellor, who can be voted out of office, is, after all, not as powerful as the former Reich President. The latter not only held office for nearly twice as long as the present Chancellor, assuming he is able to keep control of the parliamentary majority throughout the legislative period; he also had greater powers for the protection of constitutionalism under the Weimar Republic.[24] Far-reaching as the provisions for constitutional government in the Bonn Republic may be, they were conceived, above all, as a protection from a new dictatorship. Much as the permissiveness during the Weimar Republic should have been taken into account in the debates of the Parliamentary Council, the members of that council probably had on their minds mainly the dictatorship of the Reich President and of Hitler. The fear of despotism rather than of anarchy frightened those who created, and later administered, the Basic Law.[25]

[24] Comp. Friedrich, "The Development of Executive Power in Germany" 185 ff.; Grau, "Die Diktaturgewalt des Reichspräsidenten" in Anschütz/Thoma, *Handbuch des Deutschen Staatsrechts* II (1932) 275 ff; Johannes Heckel, "Diktatur, Notverordnungsrecht, Verfassungsnotstand," *Archiv des öffentlichen Rechts* XXII (1932) 257 ff.; Harlow J. Henemann, *The Growth of Executive Power in Germany* (1934); Hugo Preuss, "Reichsverfassungsmässige Diktatur," *Zeitschrift für Politik* XIII (1924) 97 ff.; Carl Schmitt, *Der Hüter der Verfassung* (1931).

[25] Comp. Carl J. Friedrich, "The Political Theory of the New Democratic Constitutions," *Review of Politics* XII (1950), 215 ff.;

The fact that the Federal Republic has a problem of permissiveness is not surprising for another reason. The parties dominating the Parliamentary Council and the government of the Federal Republic do not have the kind of programs that would facilitate determined efforts against anarchical trends.

This is evident in the case of Christian parties. We do not want to base this opinion on Nietzsche's attack upon the ethics of Christianity [26] and doubt whether such parties are in fact able to govern. Furthermore we do not want to assert that Christian parties are contradictions in terms because as institutions established by the Basic Law [27] they aim for political and temporal power, whereas the empire of Christians is not of this world (John 18:36) and Christians are supposed to forgive, even to love, their enemies (Luke 23:34; Matt. 5:44). Although the idea of Christian parties could make Christians even more desperate than the thought of Christian churches made the young Nietzsche, Christians could find consolation in Guardini's answer to Burckhardt, that power is not bad by definition; it depends upon who exercises it.[28] Nevertheless, the inherent weakness of Christian parties to govern must not be

---

John F. Golay, *The Founding of the Federal Republic of Germany* (1958); Peter H. Merkl, *The Origin of the West German Republic* (1963). The debates in the Parliamentary Council are described in *Jahrbuch des öffentlichen Rechts* I (N.F. 1951).

[26] Friedrich Nietzsche, *Der Antichrist* (1902).

[27] Basic Law, art. 21. Comp. Gerhard Leibholz, "Zum Parteiengesetz von 1967," in Horst Ehmke, Carlo Schmid, Hans Scharoun, eds., *Festschrift für Adolf Arndt* (1969) 179 ff.; Henning Zwirner, "Die Rechtsprechung des Bundesverfassungsgerichts zur Parteifinanzierung," *Archiv des öffentlichen Rechts* XCIII (1968) 81 ff.

[28] Jakob Burckhardt, *Weltgeschichtliche Betrachtungen* (Kröner ed.) 97; Romano Guardini, *Die Macht* (1951) 19.

overlooked. It derives not only from Christian ethics, but also from the organization of Christian churches. Ever since the church as a great, comprehensive ordering power was split up, its ordering function has subsided. Malebranche could still think of a legal and political realization of Christian values.[29] Stahl could still believe in a Christian constitutionalism. But what is the situation today, when even the Catholic church, a first-rate ordering power in spite of the Reformation, is threatened by dissolution? Furthermore, the Christian parties in the Federal Republic, composed as they are of Catholics and Protestants, because of their hybrid character contain a centrifugal element which should make governing difficult, to say nothing of the split between the two official parties, the Christian Democratic Union and the Christian Social Union. The historic merit of these parties in the creation, consolidation, and recognition of the Bonn Law State should not be denied. On the other hand, these achievements probably can be attributed mainly to the personality of Konrad Adenauer. Having grown up in the Empire, he still recognized clearly the importance of State Law for the preservation of constitutionalism. A leading politician in the Weimar Republic and a victim of national socialism, he not only was wary of elements inimical to constitutional government, such as nationalism and socialism, but also was in a position to counter anarchical behavior. On the other hand, all those who seek forgiveness for their activities in the Third Reich might find it hard not to forgive, in a Christian way, those who jeopardize constitutionalism in the Federal Republic.

The situation is not much different in the case of the

29 Comp. Schmitt, *Politische Romantik* (2d ed. 1925) 24.

Free Democrats. Among modern *Weltanschauungen,* that of liberalism probably is the most fragile. In distinction to clericalism, liberalism, being a reaction to clericalism, can hardly find support in the religious sphere, as the shortlivedness of liberal "religions" such as those of the French Revolution and that proposed by Mazzini has proved again and again.[30] Moreover, liberalism, having come about as a reaction against temporal absolutism, finds little support in authority, be it monarchical, nationalist, or socialist. For the liberal, the measure of all things is not God, king, fatherland, or class, but man.[31] Only man, and man alone, is an all-in-all. This omni-recognition of man basically is incompatible not only with the omnipotence of the state, but with the power of the state in general. As a result, there is inherent in each liberal the danger of undue permissiveness. Men who want to be free and, in the belief that that government is best that governs least, prefer a night-watchman-state, run the risk of falling asleep during their nightwatch, of giving up that minimum of state-power which is necessary for an orderly community life, and of waking up in a state of anarchy. This anthropocentric attitude results in a pluralistic society in which individuals dangerously swirl around like atoms, destroy the forms created by law, and end up in a war of all against all. Easy as it is for liberals to recognize the degeneration of good police into bad, they will find it difficult to recognize the merits of the good police. Fortunately, the close connection between liberal-

[30] Comp. Voegelin, *The New Science of Politics* (1952); John F. Hayward, *Existentialism and Religious Liberalism* (1962).

[31] For the meaning of Protagoras's sentence in Germany, comp. Federico Federici, *Der deutsche Liberalismus* (1946).

ism and rationalism again and again has caused liberals to think in rational terms and to see the necessity of State Law for the protection of constitutionalism. This need was also recognized by the Free Democrats in Germany after World War II.[32] On the other hand, they constantly fell prey to their inherent temptation of overlooking anarchical tendencies. It would not be surprising if inside the Free Democratic Party such trends would gain the upper hand and make that party a hybrid which, while favoring freedom in an orderly community, would be unduly permissive toward demonstrations which destroy that community.

What, finally, concerns the Social Democrats, the danger of both despotism and too lax an execution of the laws, is probably greater with them than with the other parties. What was said about the special threat to constitutionalism from social democracy, also applies to the Social Democratic Party of Germany. Furthermore, the question arises whether Social Democrats can really want constitutional government and the law that guarantees it. Since they emphasize social rights over liberal ones, must they not, in view of the incompatibility of both types of rights,[33] reject constitutionalism and be interested in the dissolution and ruin of any law which contains constitutionalist features? At any rate, ever since the founding of their party, Social Democrats, under orthodox as well as revisionist programs,

[32] The party's program of 1949 speaks of a "libertarian order of society" as the party's purpose. Comp. the remarks of Thomas Dehler on the formulation of art. 81 of the Basic Law. *Jahrbuch des öffentlichen Rechts* I (N.F. 1951) 592 ff., 605 ff.

[33] Fechner, *Freiheit und Zwang im sozialen Rechtsstaat* 5; Rumpf, *Der ideologische Gehalt des Bonner Grundgesetzes* 27 ff; Leibholz, *Strukturprinzipien des modernen Verfassungsstaates* 15.

have attacked liberalism. They have thus shown that they care little about the genuine Law State and that they can only profit from disorder in such a state. As an opposition party in the Empire, they generated disturbances until the revolution of 1918. In the Weimar Republic they shared, as a member of the governing coalition, the responsibility for the permissiveness which in the end led to the national-socialist revolution. Their vote against the Enabling Act of March 24, 1933—a courageous feat which should never be forgotten by the friends of constitutional government—appears like a late remorse for previous failures to recognize the importance of enforcing the law for the sake of that government, a last, but futile, stand against national-socialist perversions of constitutionalist residues. After World War II, the Social Democratic Party renounced Marxism in its Godesberg Program. However, this hardly solved the problems described. For that program, motivated in a large measure by the desire to get votes, does not put social rights behind liberal rights. It makes obvious how disputed the renunciation of Marxism is within the party.[34] As a party favoring a reform of criminal law, an enlarged right of demonstration and a lower voting age, the Social Democratic Party probably will remain a disturbing party in the Federal Republic. It is unlikely to oppose anarchistic pressures,[35] if only in order to undermine the liberal features of the Basic Law and to take advantage of the resulting murkiness for making

---

[34] This was evident again at the party's convention in Saarbrücken.

[35] The Social Democrat Peter von Oertzen was appointed minister of culture by his party, after having urged students "to experiment with uprisings." Recently, the mayor of Munich, Vogel, opposed anarchical tendencies within his party.

use of the general social clauses of that law [36] and for bringing about an authoritarian social order.

The described inhibitions of the parties ruling the Federal Republic and the recognition by these parties of the necessity to maintain the Bonn Law State, can lead to peculiar results. A party's official respect for the Basic Law does not necessarily amount to much. For it may mean an allegiance to that law's provisions for order as well as to those reflecting the fear of too much order, a fear that was prevalent in the Parliamentary Council. Of course, one could say that the law is wiser than the lawmaker [37] and merely take into account the protection of constitutionalism through Bonn law as it is written in black on white. However, this might prove to be difficult owing to the split personalities of the ruling parties. And then, there is always the sad legacy of the Hitler regime. Just because that regime was so terrible, many men—especially those with a bad conscience—are likely to overemphasize the fear of too much order. Thus there is possible not only a constitutionalist stasis (*Leerlauf*), due to the fact that the different conceptions of constitutionalism can neutralize each other within a given government coalition,[38] but also an stasis of State Law because within the various parties trends toward order can be cancelled out by those toward anarchy, and obligations according to law by pseudo-obligations in tune with dubious conceptions of constitutionalism. This stasis of State Law, in turn, could lead, by means of permissiveness, to an idling and sacrificing of constitutional government. That govern-

[36] Comp. *supra*, 44.
[37] Comp. Radbruch, *Rechtsphilosophie* 210 f.
[38] Comp. *supra*, 45.

ment cannot be destroyed only through formalization, but also through formlessness.

If we now consider the events in the Federal Republic during the last years, many factors point to stagnation. After having considered it over and over, the government finally made up its mind to pass emergency laws.[39] At the same time, however, reforms of criminal law were prepared which are likely to further permissiveness and potentially to bring about emergency situations.[40] Furthermore, the right to demonstrate was enlarged just about at the time when, as a result of the disorders of May 1968, which nearly brought down the Fifth Republic and certainly brought down the franc, that right was considerably restricted in France for the sake of public tranquility and order.[41] Thus the emergency legislation for the better part was cancelled out and neutralized. The idling of State Law created a public emergency, characterized by a growing criminality and by riots. This situation then created peculiar side-products such as the White Book of the Federal Government to the Spreti case, in which the government of Guatemala is held responsible for the death of the German ambassador rather than his abductors, blackmailers and murderers violating the laws of that country. Consideration is hardly given to the question whether it can be expected of a government (also from the point

[39] 17. Gesetz zur Ergänzung des Grundgesetzes vom 24. Juni 1968. *Bundesgesetzblatt* I (1968) 709. Comp. Dieter Sterzel, *Kritik der Notstandsgesetze* (1968), and the authors mentioned *infra*, note 44.

[40] 10. Strafrechtsänderungsgesetz vom 7. April 1970, *Bundesgesetzblatt* I (1970) 313.

[41] 3. Gesetz zur Reform des Strafrechts vom 20. Mai 1970, *Bundesgesetzblatt* I (1970) 505. Loi tendant à réprimer certaines formes nouvelles de délinquance No. 70–480 of June 8, 1970. *Journal Officiel* (9 June 1970) 5324.

of view of international law) to give in to blackmailers and thereby—as was first demonstrated in Brazil—to encourage further blackmail and to jeopardize the legal order of the country and the existence of its government.[42] While such a way of thinking corresponds to a leftist coalition's conception of constitutionalism and again demonstrates the risk of formal concepts of the Law State, it also shows an attitude which, in a manner endangering constitutional government, denies State Law its proper place.

The question on the future of the Bonn Republic is thus a disturbing one. Whereas previously men were optimistic, in recent years more and more voices have spoken of the uneasiness in West Germany. Just as earlier the advantages of Bonn over Weimar were emphasized, soon the question was asked whether the Federal Republic would not, after all, share the fate of its predecessor.[43] Most questioners thought of a re-emergence of dictatorship.[44] It would be irresponsible

[42] Comp. *Archiv der Gegenwart* (10 April 1970) 15401 ff. Friedrich Berber, *Lehrbuch des Völkerrechts* III (1964) 7; Georg Dahm, *Völkerrecht* III (1961) 177 ff.

[43] Titles such as Fritz René Allemann, *Bonn ist nicht Weimar* (1956), Paul Lücke, *Ist Bonn doch Weimar?* (1968), Hans Dichgans, *Das Unbehagen in der Bundesrepublik* (1968), are telling.

[44] Eugen Kogon, obviously still under the impression of the SS-state, speaks of a "tragic precaution" and fears "the transmutation of the spirit of liberty into the spirit of order." Eugen Kogon, Wolfgang Abendroth, Helmut Ridder, Heinrich Hannover, Jürgen Seifert, eds., *Der totale Notstandsstaat* (1965) 6. See also Hans Ulrich Evers, "Die perfekte Notstandsverfassung: Kritische Bemerkungen zum Entwurf des Rechtsausschusses des Bundestags," *Archiv des öffentlichen Rechts* XCI (1966) 1 ff., 193 ff.; Hans Schäfer, "Die lückenhafte Notstandsverfassung: Kritische Bemerkungen zur dritten Gesetzesvorlage," *Archiv des öffentlichen Rechts* XCIII (1968) 37 ff.:; Werner Hofmann, Heinz Maus, eds., *Notstandsmassnahmen und die Gesellschaft in der Bundesrepublik* (1967); Jaspers, *Wohin treibt die Bundesrepublik?*

to dispose lightly of such warnings and perhaps for no reason voice a suspicion that they are inspired by the left, although of course one also must beware of trusting someone simply because he is accused of being a leftist. Although not everyone who calls for law and order should be denounced as a reactionary or fascist opposed to constitutionalism, there are, without doubt, men in the Federal Republic who hide their animosity to constitutional government in a demand for law and order. The Law State is too important and, at the same time, too fragile an institution to lightly discard fears concerning its existence, irrespective of what the nature of these fears may be and with whom they may originate.

For this very reason, however, one must not be afraid of examining to what degree those who pose as permissive defenders of constitutionalism actually want to protect what is genuinely constitutionalist. The question must always be asked whether their permissiveness could not bring about the fall of the Federal Republic. In spite of the authoritarian German tradition, which probably grew as naively and naturally as other traditions did, and in spite if not because of the excesses of the Hitler regime, it is necessary in the present intellectual climate, which is predominantly directed against the tradition of order, to muster the courage not to go to the opposite extreme by being too permissive and thus to sentimentalize constitutional government out of existence. It is imperative to weigh things objectively and to resist permissive perversions. One must not be afraid of carrying out that degree of law which is necessary for the existence of constitutionalism. In doing so, one by no means becomes an opponent of the Law State. Quite to the contrary: one only follows the great advocates of that state. For these idealists always were realistic enough to recognize the value of law and order for constitutional government.

III

However State Law may have oriented the Law State, it always was indispensable for the protection of constitutionalist elements.

Friends of the Just State need not prove their case the easy way by ignoring the Third Reich and by simply disposing of it as an unjust state. Although it is true that the Hitler regime generally annihilated constitutional government, there existed even in that regime constitutionalist remnants. For one cannot very well denounce as opportunists all those learned jurists who considered the Third Reich a Law State.[45] This not only confirms Triepel's opinion that the idea of that state is older than the term itself;[46] it also shows that this concept is timeless in so far as even under the most ruthless police state not only the idea, but also institutions of constitutionalism, may remain alive. Of course, Carl Schmitt went too far when, commenting on the proceedings against those accused of setting the Reichstag on fire, he maintained as late as March 1934 that the national-socialist state was "without doubt, an exemplary Law State."[47] On the other hand, it cannot be denied that these proceedings, denounced by National

[45] A survey can be found *supra*, 36 f.

[46] Triepel, *Veröffentlichungen der Vereinigung der Deutschen Staatsrechtslehrer* VII (1932) 197. Comp. also Menger, *Der Begriff des sozialen Rechtsstaats im Bonner Grundgesetz* 6; Forsthoff, "Begriff und Wesen des sozialen Rechtsstaates" 15.

[47] Schmitt, "Nationalsozialismus und Rechtsstaat" 716.

74

Socialists and Schmitt alike, were guided by constitutionalist considerations and that such considerations up to the death of President von Hindenburg played a greater role than has often been asserted.

This raises the question whether the purge of June 30, 1934, can be considered an attempt to save constitutionalist principles by an application of State Law. Of course, in asking this question, we do not have in mind the formal "national-socialist Law State," [48] but genuine constitutionalist features. We might as well remind ourselves of the fact that at that time many friends of constitutional government, increasingly suffering under the terror of the storm troopers, sighed with relief in the hope that now law and order would be restored. As a matter of fact, the hoped-for thermidorean reaction of the national-socialist revolution, felt by many to begin on that day, enabled some men to live a little more peacefully or to leave Germany. It would be a mistake, however, now to draw the wrong conclusions. The action of the government may have prompted Stalin to remark that Hitler had demonstrated statesmanship. It hardly was a legitimate use of law for the protection of constitutionalist elements. Hitler did not even want to protect such elements. He was a statesman in the sense that Stalin was, i.e., a power-politician. As such, he, the National Socialist condemning liberalism, had even less respect for constitutional government than Bismarck who, while seeing to it that his laws against the Socialists were followed by social legislation, largely relied on the National Liberal Party. On June 30 Hitler did not,

[48] Lange, *Vom Gesetzessstaat zum Rechtsstaat* 3; Schmitt "Nationalsozialismus und Rechtsstaat" 716 f.; "Was bedeutet der Streit um den 'Rechtsstaat'?" 199.

as Schmitt asserted, protect the law,[49] but only the law in the sense of the formal national-socialist Law State. He had fallen prey to the abstract-normativistic sophistry Law State equals State Law,[50] for he identified his own law with constitutionalism. *L'état des lois, c'est moi*. He was only interested in a consolidation of his power. The argument that his action objectively served the preservation of constitutionalist elements and that the end justified the means can be countered by saying that the latter principle is dubious, that procedural guarantees are an essential ingredient of constitutional government, and that one cannot very well serve that form of government by maiming it. Furthermore, Hitler's aim was not even a legitimate one. For with the leaders of the storm troopers who opposed the Just State, there was liquidated the most important institutional guarantee of that state, namely, the separation of powers, and this liquidation facilitated a later liquidation of other constitutionalist features.[51] Hitler's states-

[49] Carl Schmitt, "Der Führer schützt das Recht," *Deutsche Juristen-Zeitung* XLIX (1934) 945.

[50] Schmitt, "Was bedeutet der Streit um den 'Rechtsstaat'?" 200.

[51] Schmitt, "Der Führer schützt das Recht" 946 f.: "The true leader is always also a judge. From leadership follows judgeship. . . . It was characteristic of the blindness of liberal statutes toward justice, that one tried to make criminal law the great charter of license, the 'Magna Charta of the criminal' (F. v. Liszt). Accordingly, constitutional law would become the Magna Charta of those who want to overthrow the government and of traitors." After referring to the state emergency law proposed by Häberlin in the 18th century and to the *acte de gouvernement* described by Dufour in the 19th century, an act which permitted emergency law even in the liberal Just State, Schmitt continues: "In a state ruled by a leader, however, in which the legislature, the executive and the judiciary do not, in contrast to the liberal state, skeptically control each other, an action by which the Führer proved his supreme leadership and supreme judgeship, must be incomparably more just than an 'act of government.' *Ibid.* 948. As to equalization (*Gleichschaltung*), see *supra*, 36.

76

manlike vision thus exhausted itself in a long-range planning of the destruction of constitutional government, regardless of how his action on June 30 may have been beneficial to that type of government in the short run. The national-socialist terror was postponed in order to become evident in an even more terrible way after the "crystal-night" and the beginning of the war.

To be defensible, actions in the name of the law must not endanger, but serve, constitutionalism. We thus approach another disputed chapter of German constitutional history, namely, the dictatorial power of the Reich President. Dangerous as Article 48 of the Weimar constitution, permitting the exercise of such power, could become, it perhaps was necessary for the protection of constitutionalist features.[52] Although we find ourselves unable to follow Schmitt's comment on the action of June 30, he was not totally wrong when he spoke of the "empty legality of an untrue neutrality" of the Weimar constitution and complained of the "inner contradictions of the Weimar system which in this neutral legality destroyed itself and delivered itself to its enemies."[53] The Weimar Republic not only suffered from an idling of constitutionalism because nationalism and socialism competed with liberalism, but also from the latter's degeneration into a permissiveness which endangered the legal order in its own way. Those who could talk with the former chancellor Brüning, know how hard he, a friend of constitutional government, must have tried to use State Law for the protection of constitutionalist elements, how he nearly despaired over

[52] Comp. Anschütz, *Die Verfassung des Deutschen Reichs* 267 ff., with a rich bibliography.
[53] Schmitt, "Der Führer schützt das Recht" 945.

the question whether during his administration such law was applied correctly and not excessively, and how again and again he answered that question in the affirmative.

It will here be left open as to whether article 48, amply used by both Ebert and Hindenburg, during the republic's birth-throes as well as in her agony of death, was the ideal provision for the maintenance of law and order. Perhaps it would have been preferable to continue the regulation of article 68 of the Imperial constitution, which provided for a clear declaration of a state of siege. Certainly, article 48 contained "a deformalization of law in a state of siege, against which *de lege ferenda,* from the point of view of a strict constitutionalist observance of procedures, important objections can be raised." [54] Furthermore, perhaps it would have been better to have understood concepts like "safety" and "order" as they were understood under the old police law with its inherent limitations. In that case, decrees to combat clear disturbances of the public order, such as crime, political excesses, attempts to overthrow the government, street riots, etc., would have been justified, but not decrees interfering with the economic and financial life, of which perhaps there were all too many. For the purpose of this essay, it is important that the friends of constitutionalism in the Weimar Republic realized that constitutional government was endangered not only by dictatorship, but also by anarchy; they saw the necessity of State Law for the protection of the Law State. [55]

The situation in the Empire was not different. Re-

[54] Anschütz, *Verfassung des Deutschen Reichs* 277.
[55] *Ibid.* 279 ff.

gardless of how constitutionalism would be viewed and be influenced by nationalism and socialism, it was generally felt that, by setting up a formal Law State, State Law guaranteed genuine constitutionalist factors. Irrespective of how much national and social outlooks would increasingly determine the law, they never absolutely pushed aside liberal ideas in the then existing conceptions of constitutional government, formalized as the latter may have been. As a matter of fact, liberal ideas generally would prevail over national and social ones. All too often would the friends of the formal Law State, having grown up in a liberal atmosphere and having liked it, take for granted liberal principles in the law they favored. This way, their type of state remained, on the whole, in conformity with constitutionalism. An influence of illiberal elements might endanger constitutional government in the long run; it did not alter the general recognition of State Law as the protector of constitutionalism.

This recognition is reflected in the laws. Aside from the Imperial constitution, the laws of the member states of the German federation provided for the protection of existing legal orders, formal Law States generally approaching the material, substantive Law State.[56] It is obvious in the literature.

In spite of its statement that the individualistic idea of constitutional government had seen its day, Thoma's survey of the elements of formal constitutionalism, published in 1910, in a large measure stands on the ground of that idea. Significantly, its title is "The Idea of the Law State and the Science of Administrative Law."

[56] A compilation in K. Strupp, *Deutsches Kriegszustandsrecht* (1916).

79

While Thoma wants to see the science of administrative law oriented by the constitutionalist idea, and the administration, the state, and its law by constitutionalist principles, he presupposed for all of this a sanction by the law of the state.[57]

The situation is similar with other authors on administrative law and State Law in the Wilhelminian era. Von Sarwey, whose type of Law State—he called it "constitution state"—was based upon a liberal constitution made by men, left no doubt about "the state-power in the form of legislation, execution and administration."[58] Although Preuss attacked Sarwey's opinion that one could arrive at the law only via the state, he favored "the recognition of the personality of the state" and saw in the Law State an institution in which the "band of the law" that keeps together the "cell-texture" of the state is protected through the realization of positive laws.[59] Rosin emphasized in the very beginning of his work on police law decrees: "Law to us is the external limitation upon the arbitrary power of persons

[57] For Thoma, who confesses to believe in the "formal-juridical idea of the Law State" and who examines the effects of that idea upon "positive German administrative law," the legality of the administration, characteristic of the Law State, consists in handling "the military power, the power over finance, the police power and the power of eminent domain, the power to supervise communes, churches and corporations, the disciplinary power over officials. . . . The principle of the legality of the administration is the basis of the modern Law State, but by no means its fulfillment. It does not yet create the legislation which *exactly* limits the scope of state activity as well as the free sphere of the citizen; nor does it establish the guarantees which firmly *secure* them." "Rechtsstaatsidee und Verwaltungswissenschaft" 201, 197, 204 f.

[58] O. von Sarwey, *Das öffentliche Recht und die Verwaltungsrechtspflege* (1880) 44 ff., 49 ff.

[59] Hugo Preuss, *Gemeinde, Staat, Reich als Gebietskörperschaften* (1889) 201, 213 f.

80

by a power superior to them. This latter, ordering power which creates objective law as the total of legal norms, we use to subjectively call the law." The realization of the law made by the state is one of the chief tasks of constitutionalism.[60] For Otto Mayer, the Just State shall *"in the manner of the law* exactly determine and limit the scope of its activity and the free sphere of its citizens." Although he clearly distinguished that state from the police state, he left no doubt that the former presupposes a strict execution of the laws.[61]

Prior to the publication of his systematic study on subjective public rights in 1892 and his *The Declaration of the Rights of Man and Citizen* (1895), Georg Jellinek had published a book on statutes and decrees with a view of "permanently transforming State Law from the fluid element of a story of the state which it is hard to circumscribe, into the solid state of aggregation of a juristic discipline." [62] His theory of the state shows that constitutionalism is based upon the lawful execution of the law. This opinion was shared by most contemporary authorities on State Law.[63]

It also was shared by earlier authors, even by an idealist of constitutional government such as Lasker.

[60] Heinrich Rosin, *Das Polizeiverordnungsrecht in Preussen* (2d ed. 1895) 1, 3, 18.

[61] Mayer emphasizes that Stahl's demand, which he quotes, "refers only to the *administration.* It no longer is a demand from the judiciary, for with respect to adjudication every state, even already the police state, firmly determines the scope of its activities according to the law." *Deutsches Verwaltungsrecht* I (1895) 62. Later on, he wrote: "The Law State is the state of the well-ordered *administrative law." Deutsches Verwaltungsrecht* I (3rd ed. 1924) 58.

[62] Georg Jellinek, *Gesetz und Verordnung* (1887) vii.

[63] For instance, Richard Schmidt first discusses "state guarantees of the law" and then only "the principle of the Law State." *Allgemeine Staatslehre* I, 175, 180.

Although in 1870 he denied the usefulness of capital punishment in Germany, he said that this punishment was justified for the safety of the state, and proper whenever the state acted in self-defense.[64] In the early 1860s he had emphasized that not only the organs of the state, but also the citizens, must obey the law: "The *Just State* addresses itself to the silent virtues of men, awakens all moral energies and oppresses each rampant, degenerate power." While the citizen "cannot claim anything" from the state "but protection from arbitrariness that hurts him," he must "sacrifice" to the state "not more," but as much as, "the lust to infringe upon the rights of others." While the "order of the Law State" primarily means the "respect of the laws for the rights of the individual," it also means the "respect of the citizens for the law." The state had to give sanction to the laws.[65]

For Lorenz von Stein, who in 1864 had dedicated a work on executive power to Gneist, the Law State presupposed not only a constitutional legislation and administration, but also administrative legal procedures with their inherent obedience to, and execution of, the

[64] Eduard Lasker, *Über die Todesstrafe* (1870) 4, 7.
[65] Lasker, "Polizeigewalt und Rechtsschutz in Preussen" 44. Lasker continues: "In the *Just State*, the violation of the law is the greatest evil which must never be suffered, regardless of where it comes from. It is the supreme task of the state to undo it whenever it has occurred. The state must listen to every complaint about violations of the law, examine whether it is justified with all the proper means that are at its disposal, and do justice to a justified complaint. This is its judicial obligation. He, who conceives of the Just State in this manner and seriously wants to continue the old Prussian tradition, will without reservation answer the question, whether every person may demand a judicial decision as often as he feels his rights are violated, in the affirmative."

laws.[66] To Gneist, an admirer of English law who in 1873 also published a study on the character of the Prussian state, it was clear that constitutionalism, just as the rule of law, could not exist without State Law. Feeling that the state is *"independently* established in the moral nature of man," he did not doubt "that the activity of the state had to be concerned with the protection of the law, that this external order must be enforceable, that obedience to law and authority are the first prerequisites for human freedom." [67] Bähr's argument with Stahl, dominated by the triad law, adjudication, and execution (under primitive conditions even permitting lynch justice for the protection of the law) postulates that the state consider it "as its first task to realize the law in definite rules and forms. State and law are inseparable concepts. By realizing the law, the state realizes the first seeds of its own idea." [68]

Stahl, who in 1845 had lectured on church discipline, wrote: "The state is a Law State by giving man, as well as the various elements of the state, a firmly circumscribed and secured legal position into which no infringement according to anybody's whim (*arbitrary*

[66] Von Stein, "Rechtsstaat und Verwaltungsrechtspflege" 321.

[67] Gneist, *Der Rechtsstaat* 28, 34.

[68] Bähr, *Der Rechtsstaat* 8. "*Law* is therefore . . . identical to *freedom*. However, it is no absolute freedom. That spiritual barrier which protects the freedom of one individual against intrusions by the other individual, must, at the same time, prevent him from transgressing that barrier and from intruding into the sphere in which the other individual may claim the same freedom. . . . For a realization of the Law State it does not suffice that public law is defined by statutes; there also must be an adjudication which determines what is just in the concrete case and thus provides for an undisputable basis for the restoration of the law, wherever it has been violated." *Ibid.* 4 f., 192.

government) is admissible. Therefore, the Law State precludes every contact with individual morals. Through definite barriers and forms, it secures for the citizen an inviolable sphere against criminal and police power. It permits him total freedom of religious and political convictions and their demonstration. No less it grants definite rights and status within the state to corporations, institutions and the church. It possesses a legal, non-transgressible order for the activities of courts and agencies, a constitutional firmness concerning the power of the sovereign and the rights of the representative body." And then he writes: "It is characteristic of the Law State that it only provides for the inviolability of the legal order, but not for its substantive content which must derive from higher moral and political principles." [69] Stahl, whose definition of the formal Law State [70] became the best known, said what later on was emphasized by most adherents of constitutionalism. In a way that shows that this proponent of a Christian Law State still was influenced by liberal ideas, he made it clear that each type of constitutional government needs an order created by State Law and the undisputable sanction of that order.

IV

Although constitutionalism was a reaction to the State Law of the police state, the necessity of its protection through State Law was recognized from the beginning.

[69] Friedrich Julius Stahl, *Der christliche Staat* (1847; 2d ed. 1858) 73 f.

[70] Stahl, *Philosophie des Rechts* II, part 2 137 f.

The emphasis by Stahl and other advocates of the formal Law State upon the value of State Law is hardly surprising. Plainly, certain types of states—national, social, national-social, national-socialist—want to carry out their respective programs. But how about the liberal state, the purpose of which is the freedom of the citizen according to the principle, that government is best that governs least? This very principle answers our question. Even the most liberal state, the purest Just State, is a state with a government which must enforce the law if the state and the human freedom it guarantees are to exist. Therefore, it is not surprising that even the liberals who stood at the cradle of constitutional government recognized a function of State Law for the sake of that government.

This is evident with Mohl. His whole work, dedicated to the Law State, appears to be framed by the idea that the latter is secured by State Law. At the beginning of his career he published studies on the State Law of the United States and Württemberg; at the end, a work on the State Law of the Second Reich.[71] Favoring constitutional government, Mohl also favored the law that made it viable. However, he was a teacher of State Law who, while in his later years he tended toward the formal Law State, never forgot the material Law State that for him always remained the core of the constitutionalist idea.[72] And he always recognized the danger of permis-

[71] Mohl, *Das Bundes-Staatsrecht der Vereinigten Staaten von Nord-Amerika; Grundriss zu Vorlesungen über Württembergisches Staatsrecht* (1824); *Das Staatsrecht des Königreiches Württemberg* (1829–31); *Das deutsche Reichsstaatsrecht* (1873).

[72] Fernando Garzoni, who reproached German professors of State Law for having formalized the concept of the Just State, and who also saw Mohl drift toward the abyss, wrote: "And yet, Mohl still appears as a teacher of State Law who saw the essence of the Law

siveness. When in the 1860s he watched with concern the development of American democracy, he not only regretted trends toward democratic despotism, but also those toward anarchy.[73] Eight years earlier he wrote that state "unity" ought to have "a veto against all excesses of individual desires, thus the idea of the state should always have the last word."[74] Although one must not see in these words a confession to a deification of the state,[75] they clearly show Mohl's fear of permissiveness. In all the editions of his work on police science, Mohl emphasized "that the citizen under a constitutional government must, above all, be in a position to claim the safety of his rights and that the fulfillment of this claim is more important than the advantages of a more consequential formal sanction of state authority and of a faster administration."[76] Still, it must not be

---

State not in the form alone, as did Stahl, Bähr or Gneist, but always kept in mind the material aspect of the idea. The Just State appears as a state which must interfere only where the activity of the citizens is not sufficient. In spite of all "relativization" (*Relativierung*) Mohl, because of his 'tendency to limit the state to do only what is absolutely necessary' preserved a hard core of the material, anti-absolutist idea of the Just State. Therefore, his Just State, which he considers a moral necessity, still contains material, always valuable elements which in the further development of the German concept of constitutionalism soon were no longer honored." *Die Rechtsstaatsidee im schweizerischen Staatsdenken des 19. Jahrhunderts* (Diss. Zürich 1952) 87.

[73] Robert von Mohl, "Die Weiterentwicklung des demokratischen Principes im nordamerikanischen Staatsrechte," in *Staatsrecht, Völkerrecht und Politik* I (1860) 493 ff.

[74] Robert von Mohl, "Das Repräsentativsystem, seine Mängel und die Heilmittel," *Deutsche Vierteljahresschrift* (3rd pamphlet, 1852) 222 f.

[75] Comp. Angermann, *Robert von Mohl* 417 ff.

[76] Robert von Mohl, *Die Polizei-Wissenschaft nach den Grundsätzen des Rechtsstaates* I (1832) 32; (2d ed. 1844) 42; (3rd ed. 1866) 60 (here the addition "formal").

forgotten that in spite of his qualification of state authority and administration as means to an end, Mohl considered them necessary for securing the freedom of the individual. Although one cannot agree with an expert on police law like Wolzendorff, who commented on Mohl's ideal state, "it is the police state in all its beauty," it must not be overlooked that, while Mohl fought an arbitrary police, he favored a scientific police and wrote a work on police law which, according to Wolzendorff, assigned so many competences to the police "that its principles of police-law are not at all likely to bring about a new cultural and legal epoch, namely, that of the Law State."[77] Even a police science according to the principles of constitutional government, much as it may restrict the police, presupposes police. Mohl himself found the term "Law State" for the constitutional state he desired "not quite fitting, since *law* is only one half of the activity of that type of state; it would be better to call it 'law and police state'. Perhaps, best of all, *reason-state?*"[78] He was too reasonable to think the state could protect the law without a police.

Mohl thought like most of the liberals of his time. He had little in common with the "ministerials" who favored a strong administration in the sense of the absolutist police state. He also kept away from the "ultras" who wanted to restrict state power more than was reasonable. As a constitutionalist, he was for the happy mean. Next to Bekk and Mittermaier, he was the main

[77] Kurt von Wolzendorff, *Die Grenzen der Polizeigewalt* II (1906) 61 ff.
[78] Mohl, *Das Staatsrecht des Königreiches Würrtemberg* I, 11 note 3.

representative of the *juste milieu,* so called after an example in France.[79]

Not only Mohl and his circle, but also members of the Kantian school, left no doubt about the value of the law for constitutional government. Being even more liberal than Mohl, they saw the task of the state in the realization of the idea of the law. Even the "dignified Behr," as Mohl called the professor of State Law at Würzburg,[80] wrote a theory of the state and a treatise on

[79] Johann Baptist Bekk opposed those who had undertaken "to spread the belief that all moral bases of the existing government were void and bad and to gradually even teach this belief to the *servants* of the government, the armed forces, in order to deprive it of authority as well as of *physical* support." Of the government and the administration he said: "Just as it generally must respect the *law* (*Recht*) even though it is not written down, it must conscientiously obey the statute on every occasion. *Only if this is done,* the *people's* sense for legality is nourished and strengthened. In this respect a government often is reproached for *weakness* if, on account of a conscientious or timid observation of statutes, it does not ward off dangers to the state. However, the sentence, *salus publica suprema lex esto,* can easily lead to abuses. In order to prevent that the respect for the statutes is shaken—something that always has bad consequences—one should make statutes which in extraordinary cases give the government the necessary power or provide that in such cases the government may *legally* swerve from the rule, so that, in doing so, it still acts *within* the laws, i.e., on the basis of a legal *authorization.* Thus the government will not be forced to violate the statute *itself* and thus, in a way, justify resistance or, at least, sanction the vulnerability of the statute." Bekk considered it a "prejudice or blindness to always try to weaken the power of the government on account of the mere possibility of an abuse of that power, without thinking of the much more dangerous abuse from the *other* side. The stronger the power of the individual or of the parts, the stronger the centrifugal forces on account of freedom and the rights of the people, the stronger must be the *unitary* (*einheitlichen*) power (of the government) to preserve the whole and to keep it together." *Die Bewegung in Baden von Ende des Februar 1848 bis zur Mitte des Mai 1849* (1850) 4, 11 f., 48 f. Comp. Angermann, *op. cit.* 186 f., 194 f.

[80] Mohl, *Geschichte und Literatur der Staatswissenschaften* II (1856) 399.

police science.[81] Aretin, said to represent "the position
of the extreme liberal version of constitutionalism," [82]
might brand "what one calls welfare-police (especially
the police providing for happiness and enlightenment)"
as an obvious "infringement upon the freedom of the
citizens." Nevertheless, even he did not think one could
do without the law. His polemics against the welfare
state emphasize the state's legal purpose and stress that
the state "must protect and respect the rights of every
individual." [83]

[81] Behr, *System der angewandten allgemeinen Staatslehre oder der
Staatskunst* (Politik) (1810); *Allgemeine Polizei-Wissenschaftslehre
oder Pragmatische Theorie der Polizei-Gesetzgebung und Verwaltung.
Zur Ehrenrettung rechtsgemässer Polizei, mittels scharfer Zeichnung
ihrer wahren Sphäre und Grenzen* (1848). Comp. Erich Angermann,
"W. J. Behr," *Neue Deutsche Biographie* II, 10 f.

[82] Angermann, *Robert von Mohl* 105.

[83] Johann Christoph von Aretin, *Staatsrecht der konstitutionellen
Monarchie*, nach seinem Tode fortgesetzt von Karl von Rotteck II,
Part 1 (1828) 178 ff. The latter passage reads as a whole: "However,
by maintaining that the rule of law *and* welfare are the purpose of the
state, one assumes *two* purposes which, furthermore, really cancel
each other out. To request the rule of law from the state means to
obligate it to protect and respect the rights of every individual; to
request welfare from it, means to demand that it violate the rights of
the individual because the means by which the greatness, the power,
the prestige, the well-being of a nation are improved, as a rule re-
quire curtailments of those rights. Therefore, he who wants both at
the same time, leaves it up to the government to take its choice between two commissions and must be content if it prefers the more
glamorous one, the one with the greater content. Under the pretense
of making happy the government can exercise, as we see it daily, the
most oppressive wardship. For, first, there is no demonstration of
human activity which would not directly or indirectly influence the
welfare of the whole. Secondly, the concept of making happy is
much too indefinite to permit its interpretation to those in power.
One ruler will try to make his people the most learned, skillful and
industrious of the earth; another will want to reduce it to bread, iron
and rough manners; a third, without such good intentions, will see
happiness in the pursuit of his private interests; they all, however,
will proceed highly arbitrarily, and with the freedom of the citizens,
their interest would be injured. On the other hand, where the

Finally, as to Kant's teachings on the state, Mohl's statement that it "brings to a head the foundation of the state upon human subjectivity" and that it justifies "the egoistic isolation of the individual" [84] is probably exaggerated. Although Kant's theory has an individualistic point of departure, it hardly paves the way for anarchism. On the contrary, it sees the purpose of the state in "the greatest agreement of the constitution with principles of law . . . which our reason through a categorical imperative makes binding upon us," i.e., in securing "lawful" freedom.[85] For the sake of the legal security of the individual and the maintenance of the legal community, Kant rejects a right of resistance and gives far-reaching powers to the ruler.[86] Angermann stated: "By unconditionally subordinating the individual to the *salus publica* which according to Kant is to be seen alone in the existence of legal order, this ideal state in many respects comes closer to the authoritarian state than to the individualistic Law State." [87] However this may be, there can hardly be any doubt that also in

---

police power is restricted to handling order and security, the rights of individuals can be oppressed neither on account of a pretended or imagined, nor a true advantage to the state."

[84] Mohl, *Geschichte und Literatur der Staatswissenschaften* I (1855) 241, 243. A criticism of Mohl's critique of Kant can be found in Angermann, *Robert von Mohl* 108 ff.

[85] Kant, *Rechtslehre*, in *Gesammelte Schriften*, edited by the Royal Prussian Academy of Sciences, Abteilung 1, VI (1911) 318, 314; *Über den Gemeinspruch: Das mag in der Theorie richtig sein, taugt aber nicht für die Praxis, ibid.* VIII (1912) 298.

[86] Comp. Kant, *Rechtslehre* 305 ff., 319; *Gemeinspruch* 298 f., 303 f.; Kurt Lisser, *Begründung des Rechts bei Kant* (1922) 35 ff.; Robert Wilbrandt, "Kant und der Zweck des Staats," *Schmollers Jahrbuch für Gesetzgebung, Verwaltung und Volkswirtschaft* XXVIII (1904) 915 f.; H. S. Reiss, "Kant and the Right of Rebellion," *Journal of the History of Ideas* XVII (1956) 179 ff.

[87] Angermann, *Robert von Mohl* 112.

Kant's ideal state, constitutionalism was realized through the law.

Turning now to the Hanoverian scholars who, as students of the English constitution, helped to pave the way for constitutional government in Germany, we notice a recognition of State Law. Influenced by Kant, Rehberg complained about the absence of a great man who could be an example to the Germans. He saw in the English state an ersatz for the state of Frederic the Great,[88] which certainly did not suffer from a deficient execution of the laws. Von Berg, also influenced by Kant, and probably by Adam Smith, without doubt was interested in the restriction of state administration. Nevertheless, he considered the safety of society the main purpose of the state and assigned important functions to the police.[89] Brandes, whose description of English government shows the influence of Montesquieu, de Lolme, and Burke, wrote: "The freest state is the state in which everybody sacrifices only that part of his free activities which the maintenance of the community absolutely requires, in which consideration is given only to a stable form of government and supposed merits."[90] Dahlmann, one of the Göttingen Seven, held a professorship for politics, cameral and police sciences. He regretted the democratization of the English constitution, which he considered an example for a German

[88] Christern, *Deutscher Ständestaat und englischer Parlamentarismus am Ende des 18. Jahrhunderts* (1939) 181.

[89] G. H. von Berg, *Handbuch des deutschen Polizeirechts* II (1799) 1: "The main purpose of the state, security of the whole society and each of its individual members." See also I (1799) 133; III (1800) 4.

[90] Ernst Brandes, "Ueber den politischen Geist Englands," *Berliner Monatsschrift* VII (1786) 217.

constitution so long as the legal order of constitutional monarchy guaranteed the rights of Englishmen.[91]

V

The preceding survey shows that, ever since the inception of the Law State in the beginning of the nineteenth century, that state presupposed a sanction by State Law. Looking no longer back but forward, it hardly is necessary to inquire about the chances of the survival of the state's law. As long as there are human communities and states, there will be State Law. On the other hand, the future of the Just State is less clear. As a result of its formalization, that state can be inverted and annihilated by State Law.[92] Considering the substantive evolution of that law as the concretization of political decisions,[93] the survival of constitutional government appears to be doubtful. It is true that, by means of State Law, constitutionalist idealists, with varying success, again and again have tried to create, even under the most adverse conditions, institutions which approach their ideal. However, welcome as these attempts may have been for combating the threat to constitutional government from the power of the state, their all too permissive conceptions often brought with them a laxity which overlooked the importance of the law for constitutional government and thus endangered the latter through state impotence.

In today's Germany, constitutionalism is probably en-

[91] Friedrich Christoph Dahlmann, *Ein Wort über Verfassung* (1815); *Die Politik* (1835; 2d ed. 1847).

[92] Comp. *supra*, 25 ff.

[93] Schmitt, *Verfassungslehre* 20 ff.

dangered as much by state impotence as by state omnipotence. Prior to World War I, when, in spite of the
formalization of constitutionalism and increasing pressures by nationalist and socialist elements, the Law
State was still predominantly liberal, Thoma wrote:
"The German may harbor the idea that his nation, by
restlessly developing historical beginnings, could succeed in creating a public law which conciliates might
and right. Like the features of Roman private law or of
Greek philosophy, such a complete conciliation could
in the end last longer than the nation of its origin as a
culture-creative force." [94] If Thoma meant by "nation"
the then existing Empire, then it did not even survive
the next decade. If one understands under "nation" the
community-consciousness of the Germans, it is doubtful
whether today, a hundred years after Bismarck's unification of Germany, that nation still exists. However,
Thoma, who perhaps anticipated the end of the German
nation, probably would have put up with all that had
there only come about the conciliation he had hoped
for. But this was hardly the case and it is questionable
whether things will improve in the future.

The predominantly liberal, formal constitutionalism
of the Empire was followed by the more national-social
Law State of Weimar; [95] and the latter was followed by
the more and more national-socialistically determined
"German Law State of Adolf Hitler," [96] in which power
raped the law. The situation is not much different today
in the communist part of Germany, which all too often

[94] Thoma, "Rechtsstaatsidee" 218.
[95] Comp. *supra*, 34 ff.
[96] Frank, "Der deutsche Rechtsstaat Adolf Hitlers" 120; Schmitt,
"Was bedeutet der Streit um den 'Rechtsstaat'?" 199.

has demonstrated the words of Kurt Schumacher, a Social Democrat tortured by the National Socialists, that the Communists are red-lacquered Nazis.

While in the eastern part of Germany the law is now crushed by power, it is, in the western part, increasingly endangered by state impotence. If the national-socialist state was a higher dimension of the national-social state of Weimar,[97] then the Federal Republic appears increasingly a higher dimension of the Weimar Republic with respect to permissiveness and laxity in the execution of the laws. This may be due to the fact that the Weimar Republic was only a reaction to the not quite democratic and rather militaristic Second Empire, whereas the Federal Republic is a reaction to the despotism of the Third Reich. Perhaps the degree of permissiveness follows from the dimension of previous oppression. In that case, Thoma's hope for a conciliation of might and right could be destroyed in the Federal Republic through an either/or of impotence and law in favor of impotence, as much as in East Germany it largely has been destroyed through the either/or of omnipotence and law in favor of omnipotence. Constitutionalism could succumb to federal-republican impotence as much as to national-socialist and communist omnipotence.

The former danger derives from a misunderstanding of the pairing of power and law. That misunderstanding came about because many men, suffering under its power, saw in the national-socialist state a state of injustice and tended toward the exaggerated opinion that power is of necessity evil and detrimental to the law.[98]

[97] Comp. *supra*, 36.
[98] Comp. *supra*, note 7.

They overlook that even if one admits the primacy of law before power, law is hardly conceivable without power unless one wants to slide into the utopias of natural law. Even the liberal state, which in view of its emphasis upon law before power probably approaches the constitutionalist ideal more closely than any other state, even in its mildest form still was a (night-) watchman-state in which the existing liberal order was strictly guarded. The liberal state was not a non-state, but a Law State.

Just as there can be, for the friends of constitutional government, no either/or of power and law, there also can be no either/or of State Law and the Law State. This does not follow from the word "State Law." Its second syllable could well be a shrewd camouflage for state injustice. However, it follows from the word "Law State" which, with all its symbolic emphasis upon the primacy of the law, does not forget the state. To juxtapose the Law State and the State Law so as to make them mutually exclusive is more dubious than to do so with justice and injustice, sense and nonsense. The latter juxtapositions at least seem to be logical, although in legal and political theory, concerned as it is with humans and with what is human, one can hardly find perfect answers and thus should refrain from black and white painting. For even the unjust state can, as counter-Law State, fertilize the Law State (especially since the latter's formalization), just as counter-sense can fertilize sense.[99] Even though the Law State fights with State Law, even though the latter often deprives the former of all meaning, the Law State has little

[99] Comp. *supra*, 12 ff.

meaning without State Law. It is true that constitutional government is something fragile that can be broken by State Law. However, its very fragility demands its protection by that law.

In the English-speaking world, "Law State" and "State Law" fall under the concept of the rule of law, which Dicey, following Harrington, made well-known. This concept implies the primacy of law, of laws in the sense of English constitutionalism from Bracton to Coke, a constitutionalism which, according to Locke and even Blackstone, in spite of all emphasis upon legislative power, saw the function of the state in the protection of life, liberty, and property, and found new confirmation in America.[100] However, the concept "rule of law" also implies the conscientious and strict execution (empire, rule) of the law which serves the interest of the individual in a community and which even in the form of statutes largely corresponds to justice. The rule of law is not only the Magna Charta of the criminal,[101] but also that of the law-abiding citizens of a community.

Desirable as clear concepts such as "Law State" and "State Law," instead of the vague "rule of law," may be, they also are dangerous because they can give the impression that they are opposites. To this political way of thinking,[102] which German perfectionism can easily let

---

[100] Comp. *supra*, 9 ff.; the author's *America's Political Dilemma* 5 ff., 143 ff.; Carl J. Friedrich, "Englische Verfassungsideologie im neunzehnten Jahrhundert: Diceys 'Law and Public Opinion' ", in Bracher, Dawson, Geiger, Smend, eds., *Die moderne Demokratie und ihr Recht* (Festschrift für Gerhard Leibholz) I (1966) 101 ff.

[101] Comp. Franz v. Liszt, *Lehrbuch des Deutschen Strafrechts* (22d ed. 1919) 18.

[102] Comp. Carl Schmitt, *Der Begriff des Politischen* (1932, 1933).

degenerate into political extremism, we suggest a mode of thinking according to political science as it was represented by friends of the Law State, such as the teacher of State Law, von Mohl.[103] Especially because the law of the power state inverted and pushed aside constitutionalism, it would be wrong now to fall into the opposite extreme and ignore the importance of State Law for the Law State, and to fall prey to an undue permissiveness which all too easily can lead to a twilight of constitutional government. Measure and mean.

[103] Comp. Friedrich, *Der Verfassungsstaat der Neuzeit* vii.

CONCLUSION

THE TITLE OF this study could also be "Rechtsstaat and Staatsrecht, Staatsrecht and Rechtsstaat." Such a symmetrical arrangement clearly shows the relationship of the two versions of the rule of law: the Law State is the ideal, the State Law the real—either detrimental or conducive to the Law State.

The position of the term "Law State" as the first and the last word of the title indicates that the Just State must be the starting point as well as the end of our constitutionalist efforts, that it must furnish the framework of our legal and political thinking. This isolated, frontal position also symbolizes the basic exposure of Justice to the vicissitudes of politics. It demonstrates how in its progression toward perfection, constitutional government always will have to face new obstacles. It shows the forlornness and tenderness of constitutionalism.

On the other hand, "State Law," mentioned twice in the center of the title, appears compact and powerful, symbolizing the threat of a state's conception of justice to the Just State. It indicates how difficult it may be for constitutionalist ideas to penetrate the fortress of State Law and to conquer it. However, it also demonstrates how the mighty law of the state can give inner strength to, and bolster, the fragile Law State, exposed as it is in its frontal position.

Dicey wrote that "not so much the goodness or the leniency as the legality of the English system of government" makes up the rule of law. "When Voltaire came to England—and Voltaire represented the feeling of his age—his predominant sentiment clearly was that he had passed out of the realm of despotism to a land where the laws might be harsh, but where men were ruled by law and not by caprice."[1] There can be little doubt that to Voltaire, as much as to Montesquieu, the English constitution, dominated as it was by the common law, also was more legitimate than the *ancien régime*.[2] There can be even less doubt that the Whig Dicey, writing in the liberal era, praised the legality of that era because it supported a legitimate constitutionalism which had matured since the eighteenth century.

On the other hand, upon Dicey's death there came about a legality which increasingly challenged legitimate constitutionalism and through statutes and decrees brought about severe restrictions of the freedom of the individual. Dicey was skeptical toward this development.[3] Seeing in the sanction of the laws a prerequisite for the rule of law, he probably would have condemned today's negation of the legal order through

[1] Dicey, *Law of the Constitution* 189 f.
[2] Carl Schmitt is of the opinion that at that time the "unproblematical law" had not yet been divided up into legality and legitimacy. *Die Lage der europäischen Rechtswissenschaft* (1950) 25, note.
[3] A. V. Dicey, *Law and Opinion in England* (2d ed. 1914) xxix ff., xxxix, xliii, liii ff., lxxi ff., lxxxvii. See also Wade's introduction to the *Law of the Constitution* cxlvi ff.

100

improper permissiveness,[4] which increasingly has been jeopardizing constitutional government.

In Germany where, due to historical factors, constitutional legitimacy stood on weaker ground than in England, the legality inherent in the rule of legislation was questioned already in the Weimar Republic. Doubts about that legality reached their climax in the Hitler regime, which demonstrated the tension between the Just State and the state's justice faster and more clearly than any other Western nation. After this terrible experience, one can well understand that many friends of constitutional government became ardent enemies of State Law and indulged in craving for liberalistic utopias. Just as they wanted Hitler's "Thousand Years' Reich" to be followed by a non-empire, they wanted the negation of the Law State to be followed by a negation of State Law. This attitude, going from one extreme to the other, may be an aspect of German thoroughness; it does not demonstrate thorough thinking. The Law State is not a non-state. It needs State Law for its realization. Of course, the friends of constitutionalism always must be cautious toward the law of the state, but they cannot afford to flatly reject it. Too important is that law's legality for the preservation of constitutionalist legitimacy.

[4] Dicey, *Law of the Constitution* (8th ed. 1915) xxxvii-xlviii. See also Wade, *loc. cit.* cxliv f.

101

INDEX

103

40, 44, 46, 58–61, 64, 66,
69, 72, 77 f., 94, 101
Third Reich, 28 f., 31, 36 f.,
44, 66, 74–77, 94, 101
Democratic Republic, 93 f.
Federal Republic, 16, 37–45,
46, 61 f., 65 f., 70–73, 94
Gesetzesstaat, 33
Gierke, Otto, 11
Gleichschaltung, 36, 76
Gneist, Rudolf, 18, 26, 29, 32,
82 f., 86
Godesberg program, 39, 69
Golay, John F., 65
Goodrich, Pierre F., 56
Gotthelf, Jeremias, 31
Government (state)
activity, regimentation, regula-
tion, ix, 10 f., 18 f., 21–24,
26–28, 34–37, 43, 50, 53–
56, 78, 80–84, 84–92
impotence, 4, 7, 54–56, 59 f.,
64–74, 77, 92–96, 100 f.
omnipotence, 7, 67, 93–96
power, ix, 10 f., 23, 28, 46 f.,
50, 54, 56, 59 f., 65, 67, 76,
92, 94
Grau, 64
Guardini, Romano, 65
Guatemala, 71

Häberlin, Carl Friedrich, 76
Haensel, Werner, 17
Hahlo, H. R., 3
Hamel, Walter, 44
Hamilton, Alexander, 21, 43 f.,
56
Hannover, Heinrich, 72
Hanover, 17, 19, 91
Harrington, James, 10, 96
Haug, Hans, 42
Hayek, F. A., 10, 15, 17 f., 33,
54
Hayward, John F., 67
Heckel, Johannes, 32, 64
Hedemann, Justus Wilhelm, 44
Hegel, G. F. W., 16

Helfritz, Hans, 36
Heller, Hermann, 15
Henemann, Harlan J., 64
Hewart, Lord, 3
Hindenburg, Paul von, 75, 78
Hitler, Adolf, 29, 37, 62, 64, 70,
73–75, 93
Hölderlin, Friedrich, 59
Hoffmann, Werner, 72
Holmes, Oliver W., 17
Huber, Ernst Rudolf, 35
Huber, Hans, 62

Idealism, idealists, 32, 50, 54,
74, 92
Individual, individualism, 23 f.,
29 f., 34, 43, 90
see also Freedom
Injustice, 11–14, 30, 33, 46, 48,
57, 74, 93–95
Ipsen, Hans Peter, 41
Italy, 61, 63

Jacoby, Johann, 31 f.
Jantz, Kurt, 41, 45
Jaspers, Karl, 62, 72
Jefferson, Thomas, 43
Jellinek, Georg, 31, 39, 81
Jellinek, Walter, 46 f., 59 f.
Jennings, Sir Ivor, 11
Jones, Harry W., 11
Just State, term for Law State,
5 f.
Juste Milieu, 88
Justice, 6 f., 10–13, 15, 20, 28,
33, 37, 46, 48, 50, 55 f.,
76, 96, 99, 101

Kaegi, Werner, 30
Kant, Immanuel, 17–19, 23, 88,
90 f.
Kelsen, Hans, 33
Kennedy, John F., 62
King, Martin Luther, 62
Klein, Friedrich, 40, 45
Koellreutter, Otto, 37

105